DISCI▮▮▮E

FOR HOME AND SCHOOL

FUNDAMENTALS

EDWARD E. FORD

Creator of the Responsible Thinking Process

http://www.responsiblethinking.com

How the Responsible Thinking Process,
properly used, provides opportunities for
educators and parents to teach students
how to look within themselves,
decide the way they want to be,
and restructure their own lives
so they can get what they want
without violating the rights of others.

Foreword by William T. Powers
Originator of perceptual control theory
Author of *Behavior: The Control of Perception*

Brandt Publishing

Cover Design: Dorothy Ford Johnson, Phoenix, AZ
Cover Photograph: Eric Johnson, Phoenix, AZ
Design & Typesetting: Greg Williams, Gravel Switch, KY
Printing & Packaging: O'Neil Printing, Phoenix, AZ

ISBN 0-9616716-9-6

Library of Congress Control Number: 2004091767

Printed in the United States of America

5   4   3   2

Brandt Publishing
10209 North 56th Street
Scottsdale, AZ 85253
480-991-4860

Contents

To Dave Anderson
    Scott Bogner
    Jack Foster
    Al Kullman

Four school administrators, who, each in his own way, have contributed so much to the development and growth of the Responsible Thinking Process. I can't thank them enough.

And to Erin Powell

She has taken special education to new levels by showing with the use of RTP how both mildly and severely disabled students can live more responsible and successful lives.

Acknowledgments

It has been over ten years since George Venetis, now my close associate, was an assistant principal at two schools in the urban center of Phoenix. After hearing me speak at a conference, he invited me to come to his schools and try out what were then just my ideas about school discipline. Today, the Responsible Thinking Process® (RTP®) is in hundreds of schools in the United States, as well as in Australia, New Zealand, Singapore, and elsewhere. As a result, I have met and worked with hundreds of educators whose dedication to children holds the highest priority in their work lives. I appreciate their confidence in me and their many suggestions for improving RTP, as well as those of Bill Powers, the creator of perceptual control theory. This book is dedicated to five of the many educators who have contributed so much.

Only time will tell how revolutionary this process is. All I know is that through the proper use of RTP, many educators have been able to teach children how to succeed, and, in the process, the educators have found within themselves an enhanced sense of worth and fulfillment. *Their own lives have taken on new meaning.*

It took me ten years to fully understand how this profound change takes place in human beings as they work through the internal conflicts with which they struggle. This change and how it actually occurs in all of us are the subjects of this book.

Edward E. Ford
Phoenix, Arizona
May 13, 2004

Foreword

This book represents another stage in the development of Ed Ford's remarkable Responsible Thinking Process. There have been many versions of this process, each building on the previous one and on experience with application to real students in real schools. Unlike some approaches that have scarcely changed in the past fifty years, RTP has faced its failures as well as celebrating its successes, and the failures have led to new insights and ultimately to a better process. This is not likely to be the last new development, either.

In its basic organization, RTP is about teaching the human beings in school systems (and many other places as well) how to get along together through mutual respect, understanding of their own human nature, and simple procedures for handling conflicts. It is a "discipline" process, but the discipline in question is mostly *self*-discipline. It is self-discipline that strengthens and frees a person rather than making the person struggle against himself or herself —or against other people.

Notice that I haven't said that this school discipline process is concerned primarily with getting students to "behave right." It is a process for all the human beings in the school system: students, teachers, administrators, security people, lunchroom aides, bus drivers, and parents. When the word "respect" is used, it is used to describe how students should treat teachers, but also to describe how they should treat each other, and how they should expect to be treated by teachers and all the other adults involved. Respect is simply recognizing that each person controls his or her own life by acting in whatever ways will satisfy all the desires and goals the person has. And truest respect arises when one realizes that it is rewarding, pleasant, and satisfying to see others in control of their own lives, so *respect becomes a gift to others that is returned again and again from every side*. Everyone in an RTP school changes, and those changes bring about a new kind of social interaction that is, in most cases, a vast improvement over what went before it.

In this latest book in Ed Ford's series on RTP, the focus is on *change*. How do people change their ways? What are good ways to make change possible? In particular, how should the key person in the RTP system, the teacher in the Responsible Thinking Classroom or RTC, deal with students sent there to think about their infractions and to plan how to avoid them in the future? It was seeing a poorly run RTC that got Ed Ford to ask these questions, and this book is the result of his cogitations and enquiries that propose some answers.

I am proud to say that Ed Ford became interested in my ideas about human organization, now called "perceptual control theory," and adopted them into his work, well over twenty years ago—and that he still finds them useful. Our collaboration over the years has made this theoretician a more practical person, and I like to think it has made Ed show signs of thinking like a theoretician (though he might deny it). The RTP process, as a result, has what I think is a sound foundation in a basic theory of human nature, while maintaining the proper position of real-life experience as the ultimate guide for theories.

William T. Powers
Durango, CO
March 18, 2004

Chapter 1
How and Where Learning to Be
Responsible Actually Happens

One of the least understood phenomena of the Responsible Thinking Process (RTP) is the eventual turnaround of some of the most difficult chronically disruptive students. Obviously, it has worked well with the less difficult students, but it is with the very tough students that a "convincing" change is seen. Traditionally, there is a tendency to describe these tough-to-deal-with students in terms of their backgrounds: the chaos in their homes, poverty, single-parent families, drug and alcohol problems, and/or abusive parents, or, at the other end of the scale, pampering with too much money, lack of interactive (quality) time (see Appendix 4) with their parents, and not enough insistence on following the rules of wherever they are. *Yet is it really their environments that "cause" students to disrupt?* Focusing on environmental "causes" of disruptive behavior and pointing to such "causes" as having little possibility of changing is perhaps a way to absolve educators from teaching students to deal within themselves.

Perceptual control theory (PCT), the theoretical framework that supports RTP, suggests alternatives for trying to deal with "causes" of disruptive behavior. (See the articles about PCT on the RTP web site, *Making Sense of Behavior* by William T. Powers, and Chapter 6 of this book.) PCT teaches that people are designed to control their perceptions, and that their behaviors are what they use to control those perceptions. For example, a student who is nearly late for class runs down the hall, trying to get to class on time. His behavior, running down the hall, is what he uses to try to accomplish his goal of getting to class on time. A teacher would see the running, but *not* what the student is

doing *from his own point of view*—namely, trying to satisfy his goal of being on time to class. Attempts by the teacher
to assign a "cause" to the running, without knowing the
student's goal, would be doomed to failure.

With regard to "disruptive homes," I have heard many
stories of highly successful students who came from the
same kind of environment (in many cases, from the same
family) as highly disruptive students. The bottom line is
that, like all of us, *students ultimately decide how they
want to be, regardless of where they live*. They are the cap-
tains of their own ships and are responsible for how they
create their own lives. They fashion their own beliefs and
values within themselves, then they set their priorities, reflecting how they want to be. For the disruptive students,
the consequence of their decisions is that they find themselves in a culture at school in which almost all of their
peers are succeeding, while they are not. They are constantly reminded of their lack of success on a daily basis by
being called to account for the rules and standards they violate by the adults with whom they have to deal. Unfortunately for the students, many of their goals they attempt
to achieve and many of the behaviors they use to achieve
those goals run counter to the standards and rules of the
educational environments in which they find themselves.

Most of these students are not very happy. They look
within themselves and are not satisfied with what they see,
and regardless of what it takes or whose rights they infringe
on, they use any means available to get what they believe
will give them happier lives. Unfortunately, they haven't a
clue as to how to turn their lives around. Most educators
deal with these students by trying to change what they see
them do, namely the students' *actions*. The students are
criticized, scolded, yelled at, and lectured about their failures on a daily basis. They are threatened with all kinds of
consequences, including detention and suspension from
school, by those who have the odd belief that somehow the
students will "figure out how to change their behavior" and
follow the rules once they have been deprived of being at

school. When you think about it, this is a rather strange way for a school to approach the problem of teaching children to think responsibly, by using punishment or rewards. It simply doesn't make sense.

But when it comes to academics, students are usually treated differently. For instance, many schools have a special staff position, the reading teacher. The purpose of this teacher is to spend time with students who need extra help in learning how to read well. It is rightly recognized that reading ability and successful advancement in school are closely related; there are many state and federal programs that recognize the need to help students who are falling behind in reading skills, as well as in other study skills. The important point here is that in these programs *the students are taught how to think and how to figure things out, thus enabling them to succeed*.

Unfortunately, the need for students, first, to learn how to look within themselves and reflect on how they are doing and, second, to work through the process of turning their lives around and create ways for getting along with others (adults as well as peers) has *not* received the same kind of recognition by educators. Students having difficulty in reading are sent to a reading teacher in a special classroom and are taught by someone *who helps them build the needed skills and confidence in themselves so they can be successful at reading*. But in almost all schools, there is no person analogous to a reading teacher who helps students lacking the understanding of how to look within themselves and decide how they want to be, and, when they are finally committed to following the rules, teaches them how to get what they want while respecting the rights of others. RTP's Responsible Thinking Classroom (RTC) teacher* is such a person. (See Appendix 2 for a Flow Chart that summarizes RTP procedures in schematic form.)

---

*The role of the RTC teacher in the home could easily be filled by the parents. The RTC for a child five years old or younger could be a chair situated within view of a parent but not where the rest of the family is

What actually takes place in the RTC? What makes this room so different from the traditional time-out and/or in-school suspension room, and so similar in many respects to a special reading classroom? What occurs in the RTC that leads to the phenomenal success of many chronically disruptive students?

First, consider what can go *wrong* in the RTC. I recently visited the RTC at a school where the administrators claimed to be using RTP properly but were not. The student plan had been shortened to only five questions. Furthermore, each student was called up to the RTC teacher's desk and was asked the five questions by the teacher, who wrote the student's answers on the form. The student was then asked to return to his desk and create a plan. *The entire process was controlled by the RTC teacher.*

Some of the few questions that were asked violated the integrity of the process and the theory that supports the process. One question was: "What do you think should be the consequences if you violate the rules again?" This raised the possibility of punishment as a way of attempting to con-

functioning. The RTC for an older child could be the child's bedroom. In a residential treatment center or a similar place, a specific person would be designated as the RTC teacher, and RTC locations would be designated according to how each facility is set up. For those schools unable to afford an RTC and an RTC teacher, another option, but far less desirable, is "pairing," where one teacher sends his disrupting students to a second teacher's classroom to settle down and work on a plan, and the second teacher sends her disrupting students to the first teacher's classroom. When a student indicates to the pairing teacher that he is ready to return to his regular class and negotiate with the teacher for whom he was disrupting, the pairing teacher first checks to see if his form is completely filled out, including his plan. If everything is in order, the pairing teacher sends him back to his regular teacher (or the person for whom he was disrupting). The regular teacher gives the student any needed help with his plan during this negotiating time. If the student continues to disrupt in the pairing teacher's room, then he is sent to an administrator, who decides whether to allow the student to continue working on his plan in the office or to send him home.

trol behavior, showing a complete lack of understanding of perceptual control theory. (See Appendix 1.) Instead of asking the student what should be done to him if he violated the rules again, which suggests the possibility of punishment, reflecting a stimulus-response scenario, it is better for the student to be asked to consider what happens when rules are violated. For example, the student might be asked "Are students allowed to stay in class or wherever they are if they continue to break the rules?" or "Do you think disrupting a class is fair to those students who want to learn?" A whole series of questions might be used: "Do you think students should be allowed to break this rule?" "Why do you think this rule was made?" "Would you want this to happen to you?" "Do you think it is fair to let other students do what you were doing?" Such questions ask the student to look within himself and reflect on the school rules and why they were created. Where RTP has been implemented, the student is not allowed to stay where he is breaking the rules, but once he decides to follow the rules, he can return and demonstrate his commitment.

Another question used in the RTC I visited asked "the reason for violating the rules," which sets the stage for arguments about whether the rules should have been violated and whether the reason was valid. What students have to learn is *how they can get what they want without violating the rights of others, rather than how to justify violating others' rights*. This question, too, showed a complete lack of understanding of RTP and its application in the RTC.

The operation of this RTC and how its students were treated seemed so efficient and so assembly-line-like—and so terribly *wrong*. Something was missing. When I visit a school and see an innovation, I try to think about how beneficial that innovation is for the students, and whether it improves the process *while maintaining the integrity of the process*. This visit was no exception. But while reviewing what was going on in this particular RTC, I went *much* deeper. I began to think about what was actually taking place within the students themselves and *how the RTC teacher, the RTC aide (if present), and the operational procedures and atmosphere of the room made it harder or easier for the student to function effectively.* In short, I began to think about the room's *culture*: the way the students and adults interacted, and the way procedures made it possible for students to learn how to succeed. In considering these issues, I realized that I was also moving closer to giving a more definitive answer to the question posed by hundreds of administrators: "What should I look for when hiring an RTC teacher?"

Students typically go through a series of stages when they encounter conflict within themselves and within the environment in which they find themselves. The first stage happens in the classroom or wherever the student is within the school's jurisdiction. The student disrupts and is asked the RTP questions. (In Appendix 3, the questions are summarized on a pocket-sized card.) First, "What are you doing?" asks the student to reflect on his present actions. "What are the rules (or procedures)?" is the second question; it moves him up to the level (see Chapter 6) at which he can look at his actions as they relate to what is allowed within the environment in which he finds himself, be it the classroom, cafeteria, playground, elsewhere in the school building or on the school grounds, or on a school bus. (For bus procedures, see chapter 30 of *Discipline for Home and School, Book One*, Third Edition.) Thus, by asking them what they are doing followed by what are the rules, you are asking students to reflect not on what they want (which happens when you ask "why," bringing on excuses) but on whether what they are doing is allowed within that specific environment.

The final question is "What will happen the next time you disrupt again?" This is not a threat but merely clarifies the operational procedure in a school that doesn't allow students who disrupt to remain where they are. If a student must leave, *the procedure allows him to return when he decides to stop disrupting*, providing that he makes a detailed plan for how he is going to get what he wanted while respecting the rights of others by following established rules, and that he negotiate his return with whoever was in charge of where he was disrupting.

Thus, the first stage occurs when students are initially asked the RTP questions, regardless of where they are on the school campus. The questions, as previously mentioned, ask them to look within themselves and decide how they want to be, which means they reflect on what they were doing as compared to the current rules, and decide whether to settle down and follow the rules or continue to disrupt. Most students, after a short reflection, disrupt no more and go about the business of learning.

The rest of the process was designed for those students who, when asked the questions, refuse to deal within themselves and with the person in charge. Some of these students, after a short period of settling down, disrupt again. They are then asked "What are you doing?" and then "What did you say would happen the next time you disrupted?" and "Where do you need to go now?" These students have forfeited their right to stay where they are and are sent to the RTC until they are ready to return and follow the rules. There are also a few students who simply refuse to deal with the teacher and continue to avoid dealing with the questions by offering excuses or challenging what she is asking. The teacher then asks such a student: "Do you want to work on this or not?" If the student continues to avoid answering the teacher's questions, refusing to deal with the problem, then the student is sent to the RTC. Once a student has committed to following the rules, he writes a plan in the RTC for how he is going to deal with the same or a similar problem in the future, reviews his plan with the RTC teacher, and then, when appropriate, returns to class and negotiates his return with the person who was in charge of where he came from.

The second stage begins when the students enter the RTC. They often come to the RTC angry or frustrated, or perhaps just upset with themselves. So they need time to calm down and gather themselves in a way that allows them to look within themselves, decide how they want to be, and, in accord with this decision, plan how they are going to get what they want without being a disturbance to others. In short, they need time to think, *undisturbed*. Once students have calmed down sufficiently and *are ready to work on how they are going to deal with the problem they were having prior to going to the RTC*, they ask permission to get a plan, return to their desks, and begin to struggle within themselves.

The third stage is generally the most difficult for students, and it is the least understood part of RTP. Initially, they review the questions on the plan form. These questions, developed since the process was initiated in 1994, are designed to help the students think through how they are going to deal with conflicts within themselves as well as with others in the future. They are permitted to sit quietly and take the time to look within themselves, think through how they want to be, and then create their answers based on their own thoughts as they work through them within themselves. *This time alone within themselves is essential if students are going to develop the necessary confidence to be successful. They must be allowed sufficient time to put together their own thoughts and possibly to perceive the need for help on one or more aspects of making a successful plan.*

This time is essential to students not only for dealing with their current situations, but also as a learning experience for future use. It is a time in which they undergo the process of *reorganization*, something all of us experience at various times in our lives. Reorganization is how humans are designed to deal with internal conflict. (See Chapter 6. Also see Chapter 7 of *Freedom From Stress*: "Reorganization: The Mind's Repair Kit.")

Suddenly I realized that it was this time when students are allowed to go through reorganization, this precious time when humans struggle within themselves as they try to deal with their various internal conflicts, that was missing in the RTC I had visited. It is only *after* this struggle that the RTC teacher can help. Once the student has struggled and found little success, then the RTC teacher can be seen as *the person to whom the students can turn for help in their struggles as they ponder a variety of potential solutions during the reorganization process*.

Applied properly, RTP results in *self-expression* by students—thoughts are expressed *by each individual*, not by going through the perceptions of others, as was occurring in the RTC I visited. A student reviews his innermost ideas as he struggles to reorganize his values and beliefs, and as he reflects on his priorities and whether they need to be revised as he deals with his conflicts. This is a time for being alone with oneself, for reflection, and for silence. If PCT teaches anything, it is that we can never, ever know exactly what goes on in another's mind. That is absolutely essential to the understanding of RTP. If I were to take my perceptions of how a student might express his thoughts and fashion his answer according to how I perceive its meaning and nuances, what a student has in mind and what I express could be quite different. My perceptions are mine, not his. If I were to control how his thoughts are expressed, I might become, in PCT terms, a *disturbance* to his system—in other words, someone who makes it *more difficult* for the student to achieve what he wants, and *impossible for him to experience the benefits of reorganization*. The RTC teacher should be perceived by students as a *means of control*—someone who helps them when they are ready by making it easier for them to get what they want, primarily by asking the kind of questions that would suggest avenues of thought for dealing with their conflicts.

What the teacher in the RTC that I visited was doing is similar to what a regular classroom teacher might do by interfering with a student struggling to work through an assignment. The teacher might become a *disturbance* either by rushing the student through the assignment or by completing the assignment for the student. However, if the teacher asked the student if he would like some help or worked *with* a student who had asked for help to finish his assignment, the chances are greater that the student would view the teacher as a *means of control*—as someone helping the student to achieve his goal, rather than as someone trying to control the student.

In an RTC that is run well, the student, in the silence of his own reflections, should not be disturbed by others. He should have the chance to think and reflect and be with himself, without being hurried. He can fashion his *own* thoughts, in his *own* time, and put together some ideas—many of which come to him as he struggles in the throes of reorganization—that might help him reflect more effectively in the future. As RTC Trainer Darleen Martin has said, "The critical part is this struggle alone they go through." *The struggle is absolutely essential for building their self-confidence and thus for increasing the possibility of their future successes.*

As a student struggles alone prior to working with the RTC teacher, he might come to see the teacher as someone who can help him—in PCT terms, a *means of control*, as defined above. And if he does, he might ask the teacher for assistance. But if assistance is given *before* the student asks for it, the student could experience it as a *disturbance*, making it more difficult for the student to think things through on his own in order to succeed. And, as in the RTC I visited, the assistance offered to the student might also be experienced by the student as an attempt to control him, or the student might perceive it as a way to help him alleviate the struggle he would otherwise have to go through when trying to solve a problem on his own. In other words, it would make it easier for him to complete his plan by allowing someone else to do most of the work for him that would ordinarily be part of his having to go through the reorganization process within himself. One would have to ask what he learns from such an experience. An example of this is a child who delays doing his homework until his parent helps him finish it—he has learned to manipulate his parent to save him the struggle of going through the process of doing his homework.

Struggling alone by students also prepares them for the future, in which they will experience reorganization many times when dealing with issues on their own, without the aid of an RTC teacher or anyone else. What could be a better preparation for them than the actual experience of this self-reflection process? Remember, if you intervene, you might cut short the process of reorganization, thus preventing learning from taking place. Retired principal George Venetis, an RTP trainer and associate, has many stories of students who struggled during several trips to the RTC, eventually straightening out their lives and showing competence in working on their own daily problems. These are cases where the reorganization process was not cut short by intervention and took, in some cases, several months of struggling. (See Chapter 5.)

When chronically disrupting students come to school, the main problems they must eventually resolve are how to build a belief in themselves and how to live in harmony within the various environments in which they find themselves. This is especially true for "spoiled" students who have learned to badger others as a way of getting what they want. Belief in themselves and respect for others will begin to grow as they struggle and then start to see personal success, possibly with the help of others *whom they believe care about them, will continue to work with them when they ask for help, and will not give up on them, no matter how many times they fail*. The experience of struggling and subsequent success is what builds confidence—the realization that "I can make it."

To create a situation as in the RTC I visited, where students are deprived of this valuable learning time, where there is no time for them to struggle and think on their own, strikes at the very heart of RTP; it does *not* allow confidence and belief in self to grow within students. How can students look within themselves when they are being disturbed by others? Looking within is done in the silence of their own hearts. And it is not because of punishments or other types of disturbances that students change, but rather *in spite of them* that successful students with some degree of confidence in themselves are able to rise above such annoyances. When students are left to struggle alone and are allowed to ask for help *when they see it as appropriate*, that is the kind of atmosphere in which they can learn to deal effectively with their problems and build the necessary self-confidence.

In this third stage, the RTC teacher needs to be highly sensitive to her struggling students and might step in with an occasional encouraging remark. She looks especially for signs of discouragement, frustration, or giving up. She asks the kinds of questions that let students know there is help available if they want it: "How are you doing with your plan?" "Do you want to discuss how you're doing?" "Is there something I can help you with?" In this kind of questioning, she is inviting, but also respectful of the students' decisions. She is always there, always inviting, but she is not intruding or controlling.

Those students who do not understand the plan making process, or who, because of their young age, are not equipped to deal with plan making by themselves, obviously need additional aid while creating their plans. In such cases, the RTC teacher does not impose herself on students, but rather is inviting: "Would you like some help with your plan?" She might ask a question that clarifies the meaning of plan making, such as "The next time someone tries to get you to talk in class, or the next time you need to sharpen your pencil, how are you going to deal with it without breaking the rules?" *Students should never be encouraged to work on their plans if they are not ready.* This could act as a disturbance and make things worse.

The fourth stage involves helping students review their plans *after they have struggled to create them* and preparing students for negotiations with their teachers or whoever the person was for whom they were disrupting. In this stage, the RTC teacher takes on more of a teaching role. The RTC teacher must have learned the skills and techniques needed for creating plans that are *specific* in detail, are *effective* if implemented according to the way they were designed, and have *measurable* goals built in, which allow the students to gauge how they are doing. (See Chapter 12, *Discipline For Home and School, Book One*, Third Edition.)

Reorganization doesn't always come up with solutions that are compatible with the rules of the environment in which we live. It randomly produces ideas or suggestions, and it is up to the individual to judge their appropriateness. All new ideas are best shared with others and tested against the various rules and criteria of where we live, including our own established standards. Fortunately, the RTC teacher is there as a part of the student's process, and to be of assistance. And the more the student perceives the RTC teacher as someone who cares, who believes in the student's ability to succeed, the more likely the student will work with the teacher.

The RTC teacher should always have at her fingertips all prior plans created by a student; this is why student discipline files should be kept in the RTC. Reviewing prior plans of students who have repeatedly visited the RTC is essential. Sometimes, comparing prior plans to those on which students are presently working brings up questions such as "If your plan didn't work before, how is it going to work in the future?" For special ed or chronically disruptive students, all special schedules and other RTC records and forms should be easily accessible as well. Special forms such as monitor sheets and earn-all plans, which many students have found useful in helping them to be successful, should be considered. (See pages 39 and 179 of *Discipline for Home and School, Book One*, Third Edition.)

And finally, the RTC teacher prepares the students for the next step in the process, negotiating their return with the person in charge of where they came from, whether a classroom teacher, a person who was supervising the area in which they were disrupting, or an administrator. If the negotiating experience is new to a student, such preparation might include doing a role play with the student, which would include dealing with some of the objections the student might encounter. The RTC teacher's ability to anticipate what the student might have to deal with in the future is critical for helping students.

What, then, is the overall role of the RTC teacher, according to RTP? Quite simply, *when students are ready, and AFTER they have struggled alone with all of the questions as well as their plans*, she

• teaches the students how to look within themselves and decide how they want to be and whether that is reflected specifically in their plans,

• suggests additional questions to consider and helps by using role play scenarios,

• suggests ideas that might be helpful to think about—possible alternatives to what they have already thought about—to help them with their own internal struggles, and

• supports their efforts, when they are ready, to structure their life and create effective plans to become responsible human beings.

The fifth and final stage involves negotiations with whoever was in charge of where the student was disrupting. Negotiating is a critical part of this process. When a student is negotiating his return to a classroom, the teacher must first allow the student to explain his plan. This should include an explanation of how he is going to deal with the same or similar problem the next time it occurs, including how he will deal with any unexpected difficulties, as well as specific measurable goals by which he can judge the success of his plan. If the teacher has any concerns about the plan, she should *wait until after the student has finished his explanation*. Then she can express her concerns and, if she has alternatives, offer them. Finally, *together* they work out a satisfactory compromise. A student's plan should never be ignored or refused. This dialogue shouldn't take long with the majority of students, maybe five to ten minutes at the most, but it is critical for the student to experience someone who, like the RTC teacher, is *willing to listen and take the time to help the student create a successful plan*.

In addition to the negotiations, the fifth stage involves the subsequent attempts by the student to implement his plan. This is where "the rubber meets the road": where the student attempts to test the effectiveness of his plan. Even for those many students who, for one reason or another, fail in their initial attempts to succeed, this is where they might begin to see "a light at the end of the tunnel." Surrounded by people who he believes care about him and who are committed to helping him, the student might find this caring experience sufficient to generate a hope which will eventually turn into signs of a commitment and possibly a small improvement, *allowing his belief in himself and his ability to succeed to begin to take hold*. He might not have complete success all at once, but even the slightest taste of success might be enough to convince him to continue reorganizing in the direction he is going and to stay committed even after several failures to turn around fully.

Remember, what might seem like a small gesture on our part or a small movement toward success on their part could be a big sign of hope for them. I've known several students who have worked at improving their lives for months, and some who have worked for years. Their tenacity is something to behold, but *it comes from working with those who they believe care about them and have confidence in their ability to succeed. It might additionally come from experiencing success in small increments, such as improving in one class, with one teacher, or doing one small part of an assignment successfully.*

This process, used properly and with sincerity, assures each student the best chance possible for a successful, happy, and responsible life. *It is important to remember that all of us, according to PCT, are control systems, and whatever we do does not* cause *the student to change. RTP gives the student the best chance, but, ultimately, success takes place* within *the student. The smallest, almost insignificant, changes experienced by the student and a caring relationship with others are what convince the student he can make it.*

A critical part of the support system for chronically disruptive students is the school counselor (or social worker or psychologist). It is recommended that the school counselor meet with the RTC teacher at least once a day, preferably in the morning, to review those students who were in the RTC the day before, especially the "frequent fliers" showing up repeatedly in the RTC. This is a way to keep updated both on the students with whom the counselor is currently working and potential candidates for counseling. Also, for chronically disruptive students, an Intervention Team might be called (see *Discipline For Home and School, Book One*, Third Edition, pages 92–97). The school counselor is the ideal person to head the Intervention Team, which gathers together those adults, especially the parents, who have spent time with the student and are willing to commit to providing important information and support for the student. It should be noted that the student should *not* be part of this team. Unintentional critical remarks, especially by a parent, can easily make it far more difficult for the team to serve its purpose. Also, the purpose of the team is to look within themselves and decide how they can best help the student.

Thus, with the proper use of the RTC, an effective learning process is available for those students who desperately need to reorganize their lives totally, beginning with learning to respect the rights of others, and then learning how to live in harmony within the various environments in which they find themselves. They should learn first to reflect on their priorities and then to follow the various standards and guidelines of wherever they find themselves, thus becoming responsible students as they deal with the tasks of academic learning. Good RTC teachers (and other educators, regardless of whatever parts they play in the various stages mentioned above) know where their students are in their struggles and will offer them assistance by asking the appropriate questions to help the students work through those struggles. *But the students must first go through those struggles alone before the RTC teacher or any other educator can assist them.* And assistance does *not* mean doing their work for them. *They have to be allowed to reorganize in their own time and at their own speed. The RTC teacher certainly cannot reorganize for them, and she must see evidence of their struggles BEFORE offering them help. It* must *always be kept in mind that for all individuals, real change takes place as they struggle alone within themselves.*

This struggle takes place in teachers, administrators, and especially parents, as well. As you read the various chapters in this book, you'll meet educators who've gone through reorganization, attempting to deal with various school and personal problems. It should be remembered that what comes into the mind as a result of reorganization is a possibility, not a guaranteed answer. The reorganizing parts of our minds generate new ideas, but it's up to us to look at them critically and discard the ones that probably won't work, such as when a teenager who desperately wants a new car gets the idea of stealing money to buy it. These struggles are not that much different from those of creative artists painting a canvas, redecorating a room, composing music, or writing a novel. Students in the RTC, who have already been asked about and have reflected on the rules and procedures of the school, and who will be working with an RTC teacher after they have attempted a plan, will be more likely to discard ideas suggested by the reorganizing parts of their minds that would lead them to break more rules. That is why the initial two questions ask them first what they are doing, asking them to look at their behavior or actions, and second, what are the rules or procedures, asking them to compare their actions to school standards, and even, perhaps, their own standards. They might even reflect on their own beliefs and values, if those beliefs and subsequent standards are antagonistic to the culture of the environment in which they find themselves. For example, dressing in a certain style of clothes might reflect a student's values and subsequent standards, but might not reflect the standards of the school.

Many times I am asked a question about the application of the process, and I don't have an answer—but I have confidence that an answer will eventually come to me. In short, I have confidence that my mind will figure out the solution I'm looking for if I just leave it alone and allow my brain to struggle by itself, in the same way students should be allowed to do in the RTC. In the example I gave above about the RTC, I knew something was wrong, but I couldn't immediately figure out what it was. I knew eventually it would come to me. And it did. I never suspected that it would spawn this book!

I have learned over the years that, just as the RTC teacher should allow her students time to think and reorganize in a relaxed atmosphere without rushing the solution, allowing time for ourselves to reorganize and let our brain try to solve our problems can be valuable tool for *all* of us. The more I've worked through various challenges I've confronted, the more I realize I can't really take credit for what comes out of my brain (except for those things I've learned through study and effort), because I didn't put it in there. I just let it come out. And it really is something to watch ideas flow out and to sit in awe of what the brain can do.

In the RTC, students learn to have confidence in the ability of their minds to come up with solutions, and they learn to judge those solutions based on the criteria and standards they have set and are surrounded by. And once they learn those things, they have a valuable tool they can use for the rest of their lives. When people have confidence in themselves, they have developed confidence in their brains' ability to come up with solutions, with ideas, and with appropriate goals which will help them solve problems with which they are trying to deal. The job of the RTC teacher is to offer sufficient support to her students for however long it takes until they have acquired this confidence in themselves. This is especially true for disruptive students.

And who is better suited to help these children than the RTC teacher, who teaches her students self-reflection and self-evaluation? These students learn from her these valu-

able tools in the silence of their own minds and hearts, in calmness, and without external judgment or control. The gradual internal growth in learning how to take responsibility effectively that develops within students as they reorganize within themselves and struggle to redefine and set effective values and beliefs, priorities, and standards, and to restructure their lives is *the mark of a good RTC teacher and a successful application of RTP by all those working in a school.* And, regardless of our places in life, learning how to use this reorganization tool properly and teaching others how to do the same can help all of us build more fulfilling lives.

Chapter 2
Reorganizing in the
Responsible Thinking Classroom

Darleen Martin
RTC Teacher and RTC Trainer
Villa de Paz Elementary School
Phoenix, Arizona

Life is a succession of lessons which must be lived to be understood.—Helen Keller

In Chapter 1, Ed discusses the five stages of the Responsible Thinking Process. Here, I will share some of my students' experiences in the second, third, and fourth stages. I have changed their names to protect their identities.

Keep in mind that if the RTC is operated as intended, then students will perceive it as a place where they can "just be left alone" until they are ready to talk.

The Dream Catcher

Arriving at my RTC one morning, I found Charlie, a Kindergarten student, waiting outside the door with tears in his eyes and a scowl on his face. I asked him if he was waiting to come in the room and invited him in. He immediately pulled out a chair and plopped down in it. I asked him what was wrong. He told me he was having a bad day, and he didn't want to stay at school. He wanted to go home.

"Would you like to stay here for a while and think about whether you really want to go home?"

"Yes."

"Do you want to talk to me?"

"No. I'm just sad."

"OK, if you want to talk, let me know. I'll call your teacher and let her know that you want to stay here for a while. That way she'll know where you are, and you won't be marked absent."

I called Charlie's teacher and went about my morning routine. He fell asleep for about a half hour, and when he woke up, he was ready to talk. He came up to my desk and told me he was having a bad day because he didn't sleep much the night before. He woke up because of a bad dream. We talked for a while, discussing bad dreams. If he had them very often, did he talk about them with his parents, or with his brother or sister? What did he usually do when he had bad dreams?

Suddenly, while we were talking, Charlie gasped and his eyes got really big. I almost could see a little light bulb glowing over his head.

"Ms. Martin, I know what's wrong!"

"What, Charlie?"

"My dream catcher, *it must be full!!!*"

He decided that when he went home after school he was going to take the dream catcher and shake it very hard so all the old dreams could fall out and there would be plenty of room for new dreams.

Charlie had realized that he was experiencing error, and he wanted to make things right in his world, but he needed help doing so. On his own, Charlie had come to the RTC, even though he had only been in the RTC on one previous occasion. Satisfied with his solution, Charlie skipped happily off to class.

Reorganization plays an essential role in the Responsible Thinking Process. We facilitate successful reorganization within students who are experiencing conflicts by providing a place—the RTC—for them to "just be" until they request assistance or they have resolved their conflicts on their own. The RTC teacher should allow reorganizing students to use her in their search for satisfaction, helping them *if and when they ask for assistance* during their reorganization.

In the RTC, all students and adults should be treated respectfully, according to the way they are designed as living control systems. Students in the RTC are not there so the RTC teacher can convince them or encourage them to act in certain ways. Each student must come to terms with what is acceptable in his current environment and find a way to deal with it accordingly. In the RTC, the student has the opportunity to learn to control important perceptions in responsible ways.

Students in the RTC generally show some frustration. That makes sense, because PCT tells us it is only when people experience error that they change their actions.

Mom's Hurt Hand

Dana came to my RTC with a note written on notebook paper. The note included only her name, the date and time, and the signature of her classroom teacher. There was no explanation of why Dana was at the RTC. I asked if she was there on a privacy pass. This pass is often known as a self-referral or chill-out pass, which students use when they are angry or upset and want to go to the RTC to have a place to calm down, to do their work, or just to be alone. Dana told me that her teacher thought her mother hadn't signed her progress report the previous evening, and that Dana had forged her mother's signature.

I asked, "Who actually signed the paper?" Dana explained that her baby sister had slammed a door on her mother's hand when she was watering some plants. She motioned towards the top of her hand, showing me where her mother's hand was injured. Her mother was unable to sign the report, and, according to Dana, asked her to sign the report for her.

"Then you signed the report?"
"Yes."
"Your mom asked you to sign it for her?"
"Yes."
"Did you try to explain this to your teacher?"

"Yes, but she thought I was lying."

"Were you being truthful?"

"Yes, my mom hurt her hand and couldn't sign her name."

"If I called your Mom, what would she tell me?"

"That she hurt her hand."

"Would you like me to call your Mom and ask her about this?"

"No, I don't think she is home."

"OK, have a seat and think about how this problem the teacher is having with what you are saying can be solved."

Dana sat down at a desk. I called her classroom to speak with the teacher, but the class wasn't in the room at the time. After about fifteen minutes, Dana asked if she could get a plan form. She began working on the form. When she had completed it, I asked if she was ready to go over her plan. She was ready and came up to my desk.

The first question on the form is "What did you do?" Her answer was "I lied to my teacher." I then asked, "Did you make up the whole story about your Mom hurting her hand?" With downcast eyes, she said, "Yes." We continued reviewing her plan, and we talked about honesty. I asked her if it was important to her that others tell her the truth. How did she feel when someone lied to her?

I was trying to learn about the situation *from Dana's perspective*. The best way to learn about conflict from a student's perspective is by asking questions. An understanding of the student can be sought after time is allowed for the student to sit undisturbed while dealing with her conflict and thinking things through.

RTP is an "in here" process, not an "out there" one. It is about what goes on within the person, as opposed to what is done to the person.

Anger Journal

Michael had a great deal of difficulty controlling his actions when he became upset. His usual manner of dealing with situations was by cursing or hitting. He would immediately lash out physically or verbally at anyone in his vicinity. Afterwards, in the RTC, he was always upset with himself and the ways he had dealt with his anger. I worked with Michael on various plans for five months before he came up with something that was successful for him.

Michael's favorite subject was writing. He had a lively imagination and loved to write stories. I asked Michael if he had ever tried to write about the things that upset him. He said he hadn't tried that before, but he liked the idea of writing stories and drawing cartoons about different situations that upset him. I gave him a composition book in which to do this.

During the next week, when I saw Michael, I noticed he had his composition book with him. If he saw me, he called out "It's working" and waved the book in the air.

One day during that week, he stopped by the RTC to share with me a poem he had written the day before. A girl had called him a name, and he became upset. Normally, Michael would have called the girl a name in return (making sure to one-up the insult!), or he would have tried to slap her. Instead, he wrote this in his composition book:

You are rude and you're loud
You're mean enough for two.
If I were a cloud,
I'd rain all day on you!

Michael's teacher was very supportive when Michael returned to class with his plan. She provided a desk that Michael could move to when he wanted to make an entry in his composition book.

Educators need to stand back and let the process do the work. We need to proceed at the pace set by the child. Students will only begin to succeed when they decide it is important to them.

Speed Limit Story

The RTC door opened. In stormed a student, tossing his referral in the referral tray on my assistant's desk. He yanked out a chair and sat down as he loudly stated, "It's not fair. There were others talking, too. I'm not going to write a plan! It's not fair!" His actions indicated he was experiencing a great deal of error.

At the time, I was working with a student at my desk, and there were other students in the room working on their plans. We all looked up, and I asked the student, "Jason, what are you doing?"

"I'm talking—but it's not fair! I wasn't the only one talking in the class, and she only sent me!"

"What are the rules in the RTC?"

"No disrupting."

"Jason, if you continue to yell out, and disrupt, what will happen?"

"I'll have to go home."

"Is that what you want?"

"No."

"It seems that you are very upset. Would you like to calm down so we can talk when I have finished working with Kathy?"

"Yeah, I want to tell you what happened, because my teacher was just picking on me."

Jason then put his head down on the desk. His hands were still in fists. When he entered the room, it was obvious to me that he was upset. It is very important for the RTC staff to give students space. The tone of voice is extremely important. When Jason was yelling about how unfair things were, I was especially careful to ask him "What are you doing?" in an inquisitive way, with a slight smile on my face. You need to convey encouragement, as opposed to any type of control. But Jason also did not have the right to disrupt the RTC, and the questions were necessary, thus allowing Jason the opportunity to reflect on what he was doing at that moment and the effect it was having on

others in the room. The other students had stopped working on their plans and were looking at Jason. One was
snickering. I stopped working with Kathy in order to speak
with Jason. I also let him know I wanted to hear what he
had to say by asking him, "Would you like to calm down so
we can talk when I have finished working with Kathy?"

After Kathy and I went over her plan and she left, I called
Jason up. He immediately started telling me that there
were other students talking when the teacher asked him
the RTP questions. I patiently let him tell me his version of
what happened in the classroom. It appeared that he also
needed to vent. I then asked him, "Were you talking?"

"Yes"

"What were you supposed to be doing?"

"Quietly working on our projects."

"So, if you were supposed to be working quietly on your
projects, and you were talking, were you breaking the
rules?"

"Yes, but so was Johnny, and he's not here."

"You know, Jason, I'm not saying that Johnny wasn't talking also. He might have been, but aren't you here because
of what *you* did?

"Yes."

I could tell that he was still quite upset.

"Let me tell you a true story that happened to me. One
Saturday I was in the car on my way to Tucson to visit my
sister. I was just outside of Tempe. It was a beautiful day. I
noticed that the speed limit was 75 miles an hour, but cars
were passing me. I sped up to 83, set the cruise control,
turned up the music, and got ready for a nice two-hour
drive. After about a mile, I looked up in my rear-view mir-
ror and noticed a police car with his lights flashing. At first,
I thought he must have been going after one of the cars that
had recently passed me. I hadn't driven much further when
I realized that he wanted *me* to stop. I pulled over, stopped
the car, and rolled down the window. The officer approached and asked for my driver's license and proof of
insurance. As I was gathering these items, he asked me if I

knew how fast I was driving. I replied, 'About 80, but officer, those other cars were going much faster, they were passing me!' 'Sorry miss. The speed limit is 75. You broke the law, and I can only stop one car at a time.' Tell me Jason, what do you think happened next?"

"You got a ticket?"

"Why did I get a ticket?"

"Because you were speeding, and you broke the law."

"Did it matter how fast the other cars were going?"

"No."

Nothing was said by either of us for a couple of moments, and I was wondering what he was experiencing, sitting there, talking with me.

He broke the silence with "Thanks, Ms. Martin. I'd like to work on my plan now."

I have learned through the years from experiences I have had with students that sometimes sharing a personal story about me helps the reorganization process within them.

We don't see reorganization, but the actions of it. Remember, we cannot actually "see" the reorganization going on in a child, but when Jason asked to work on his plan, I knew reorganization was going on within him because of his actions. He was now at the stage where he was ready to develop a plan.

Chapter 3
Creating a Classroom Environment That Fosters Responsible Thinking for Children with Disabilities

Erin Powell
RTP Special Education Teacher and Trainer
Creighton Elementary School District
Phoenix, Arizona

Kevin is a thirteen-year-old student with moderate mental retardation. It is common for Kevin to yell, hit, and throw things when he becomes angry. He also has a history of running away from the classroom when he became angry. If an adult tried to assist him in returning to the classroom, Kevin would attempt to hit her. On one particular day, he was asked to complete a reading assignment. Kevin was having difficulty completing the assignment because he thought another student was making faces at him. He threw a pair of scissors, yelled at the student, and ran out of the classroom. As Kevin was running down the hallway screaming, I asked him, "What are you doing?" Kevin immediately stopped, ran back into the classroom, and went to the classroom bathroom. After about ten minutes, he opened the door and asked me to come over. He was ready to be asked the RTP questions. Why was Kevin able to return to the classroom on his own without physically assaulting someone or running away? Why did this change take place within him?

I have always believed that *any* student can achieve his personal best academically and socially if his teachers have high expectations for him to do so. No matter how severe a student's disability might be, he is still a living control system just like his non-disabled peers. In other words, a child with a disability is a living being trying to control his perceptions. According to RTP, personal change occurs when individuals reflect within themselves and decide how they want to be. This is not different for a child with mental retardation, a specific learning disability, autism, an emotional disability, or a physical disability.

When working on academics with students who have cognitive and emotional disabilities, it is common for teachers to provide multiple opportunities to practice difficult skills. Teachers tend to provide a scaffold of prompts to help the students learn such a skill successfully. Furthermore, they teach the skill in context so that the skill is meaningful. For example, Kevin is learning to count coins up to a dollar. When there is a bake sale, Kevin is able to buy baked goods. Initially, he had difficulty giving the sales person fifty cents. The teacher gave him a coin card that modeled to him what fifty cents looked like (two quarters). The next time he purchased a baked good, the teacher needed to give him verbal cues. Kevin practiced this skill until he knew that two quarters are equal to fifty cents. He was able to practice the skill in a context that was meaningful to him. As teachers, we help students with academics in this way naturally. The same should apply to teaching social skills.

Because a child with a cognitive or emotional disability tends to have more difficulty with learning new skills, it is important for a teacher of such students to arrange the classroom environment so that the students feel secure to struggle when they have internal conflicts. There are three ways a teacher can structure the classroom environment to support the students.

The first way is to develop and teach classroom rules. The foundation for learning any social skill in the school setting is to have classroom rules. In order for students to view these rules as meaningful, they should be allowed to help develop them. Furthermore, their struggles to find solutions will be easier if they agree upon the rules. They are involved with the process of how they want their classroom community to operate. It is also important that the students receive multiple opportunities to practice these rules on a daily basis. This could be done through role playing, giving both examples and non-examples of rules, and describing specific incidents that exemplify classroom rules. This gives them the practice they need to become successful socially. Kevin probably went back to the classroom after he was asked "What are you doing?" because he had a vested interest in the classroom rules. He knew that he could begin to struggle with his conflict (reflecting upon his actions and how they relate to the rules) in an environment that allowed him to do so, instead of running away. Because he helped develop these rules, he had a better understanding of the reasons for having the rules.

The second way a teacher can foster a classroom environment where students feel comfortable to struggle internally with their conflicts is by allowing places and times for those struggles to occur safely. Instead of running away, Kevin went into the classroom bathroom and closed the door. He chose to go to a quiet place (the bathroom) to reflect upon his conflict. He was allowed to stay in there without any adult interruptions as long as he was not hurting himself or others. After ten minutes, Kevin came out of the bathroom and asked for help. Allowing Kevin to have this time was crucial. This quiet time without disruption allowed Kevin a safe place to reflect upon his actions and how they relate to the classroom rules. He needed this time as the critical part of his reorganization, which began with the question in the hallway and led to his looking for help from someone he trusted. My job was to have the patience to allow Kevin to get to this stage by allowing him to struggle in a quiet and safe place.

The third and final way a teacher can arrange the classroom environment to assist students in becoming responsible thinkers is by being part of a support system for the students. Asking the RTP questions in an appropriate way assisted Kevin in arriving at a more favorable outcome than running away. Later, when he left the bathroom, Kevin let me know he wanted my help by asking me. Students with severe disabilities have a more difficult time than other students with higher-order thinking and communication skills. That does not mean they cannot think critically, but they need more support with organizing their thinking, coming up with solutions, and expressing their thoughts. It is important that teachers do not try to help students by thinking for them. When a student is ready to work on his plan, the teacher should act as a facilitator by helping the student reflect upon his actions and guiding him in developing a solution. By allowing students to come to you when they are ready for support instead of forcing yourself on them, you will find that they will be more likely to use you for support.

Billy is a twelve-year-old boy with autism. He has a difficult time expressing himself. He likes to imitate other students, especially Kevin. When Kevin yells out an obscenity, Billy will repeat the words over and over. When Billy was asked the initial set of questions for such a disruption, he needed the questions to be rephrased into yes/no questions. This was because he has a difficult time understanding the meaning of the questions. For example, the teacher asked "What are you doing? Are you saying bad words?" He also needed visual cues to help him answer the questions. When the teacher asked "What are the rules?" Billy answered the question by pointing to the classroom rule chart that has pictures paired with written rules. The teacher became the facilitator for Billy by providing him with the opportunity to express himself. It would be easy for the teacher to tell Billy what he was doing, especially since Billy likes to imitate other people. Instead, the teacher allowed Billy to express his *own* thoughts by providing the support Billy needed to organize and express his thoughts.

Another important component of support systems for students is developing relationships with students that are based on mutual respect. Such relationships can occur naturally when you follow the RTP process appropriately. It is important to model for the students how to treat one another. By asking the RTP questions in a calm voice, the teacher models for the students how to treat others when they need help. By teaching students how to follow the rules and allowing them to be a part of how this happens, the teacher is setting expectations and modeling how the classroom environment needs to be in order to establish a safe learning environment. By providing a safe place and uninterrupted time for students to reflect upon their actions, the teacher is modeling patience. She is also showing the students that she believes in them. She believes that they can be successful at making the appropriate choices.

I was recently sent to a classroom where yelling, punishing, and threatening students was a common response to disruptions. When I walked into the room, I felt it was an unhappy place to be. Relationships were not being developed, because the adults and students were constantly fighting. Moreover, the teacher was modeling inappropriate ways to interact with others. If an adult walked in and said "Hi" to the students, it was commonplace for the students to make rude gestures or comments to the adult. Sometimes they would ignore the adult's greeting and walk away. Needless to say, learning was not happening, because the adults were too busy punishing students for disrupting. I was asked to come in to help the teacher and students. I provided help by establishing classroom rules with the students and staff, teaching the rules to the students on a daily basis, implementing RTP, and teaching the adults how to utilize the process appropriately. I was in this classroom three days a week for six months. Yelling, threatening, and punishing did not occur during this time. Instead, a schedule was developed so the students had time to discuss and practice the classroom rules. The teacher and classroom aides were trained to implement the RTP procedures appropriately. This included learning how to ask the questions, how to help students develop plans, and how to negotiate the plans. At the end of this training, it was amazing to see the difference in the classroom. The students who previously greeted me inappropriately would now run to me and give me hugs. This was because mutual respect was taught and modeled; therefore, positive relationships were developed.

Students with disabilities need sufficient practice time, scaffolding of prompts, and the opportunity to learn skills in meaningful contexts in order to be successful with learning new concepts. The more severe the disability, the more support they will need, because these students have difficulty with higher-order thinking and communication skills. Many teachers feel that they need to wave their magic wands and "fix" the students. This is not our job, nor is it possible. If teachers continually try to impose themselves on their students, then the teachers will become disturbances. Instead, teachers need to create non-threatening learning environments where rules are established by students, practiced on a daily basis in meaningful contexts, and supported by a variety of cueing systems. Furthermore, teachers need to provide space where students can feel comfortable to reflect upon their conflicts. Positive relationships need to be developed where the students feel the teachers provide support systems and are not disturbances. Whether they are experiencing an academic struggle or a social struggle, children need to look within themselves and decide how they want to be. As teachers, we can assist them by arranging the environment so they have places to feel comfortable doing this.

Chapter 4
The Struggle to Reorganize by Students and Educators

Al Kullman
Principal
Evart Middle School
Evart, Michigan

and

Scott Bogner
Principal
Evart High School
Evart, Michigan

Using RTP has allowed us to focus on those students who need attention and to provide them with ongoing support for solving their own internal conflicts. Students in conflict soon come to the attention of the RTC teacher. If the RTC teacher begins to see a particular student visit the RTC frequently, it suggests that the student is in conflict. Such students are trying to deal with their conflicts; when we see indications that they aren't making progress, an intervention is called to help us find ways to provide more support for them.

When we give presentations to educators who are desperate for an approach to discipline that works, we often talk about students who, after having been "frequent flyers" in the RTC, start to turn their lives around. In these success stories, we discuss the relationships RTP has helped us build with these students, and how we must constantly work to develop and maintain relationships that our students can count on. One example is the story of Karen, who is definitely a "work in progress." While in our middle school, she was a frequent flyer, and once she stayed in the RTC for an entire month during her math class because of a conflict with the math teacher. Interventions were called, but Karen's alcoholic mother never attended, and so we just kept trying to support Karen, using the process. Little did we know that Karen would have problems with alcohol, too, and that this episode was an indication of the internal struggles she would deal with as she matured. After a month in the RTC, Karen suddenly decided to go back to math class. What had happened? There were no magic words or potions, no healing powers bestowed on her from above, and no punishments given to try to change her behavior (our experiences tell us this would have only made things worse). Why did Karen decide to go back to class? She had eventually stopped struggling through reorganization, but only after having the necessary time to look internally, reflect on her present standards and priorities, and decide how she wanted things to be. The time required for this depended solely on her; it had nothing to do with how long the adults involved thought it should take. Her reorganization did not cure *all* Karen's problems, but it did seem to help with the conflict she had with her math teacher. It also taught her a lesson in dealing with conflict that she might be able to use more wisely in the future.

When we first started working with RTP in our schools, we had very little understanding of the concept of reorganization. We realized that people sometimes struggled and went through hard times in their lives, but we never really looked in detail at reorganization as described by PCT. Before RTP, when a student experienced conflict, we just thought the student was being disrespectful or obstinate. We thought if we did something to a student, then the student would magically start behaving differently. As we learned more about the process and the theory behind it, we realized that students—like Karen—reorganize when they experience conflict, and that reorganization happens *with or without* our intervention. Ultimately, we changed the way we deal with students in conflict *by allowing them to deal within themselves effectively while not allowing them to disrupt the learning environment*. But before we could make that change, *we* had to reorganize. Dealing with Karen's struggle started the reorganization process within us.

We have been intimately involved with RTP for about six years, and both of us have come to realize that we have just scratched the surface with our own understanding of RTP and PCT. We now constantly refer to PCT as we apply the teaching of RTP. We believe it is fundamentally important that RTP be tied to the theoretical basis of how our brains work. Doing this has helped us protect the integrity of RTP, and it has profoundly changed the ways we think about and deal with both students and adults. Both of us have arrived at similar ways of thinking, although our backgrounds are quite different.

Al had been exposed to RTP while working in an alternative school and was largely responsible for bringing the process to Evart Public Schools. He was able to pilot the process in his middle school during a period of administrative change and saw tremendous results. His building was calmer, and there was less yelling by both students and staff. Students were not lined up in the chairs in Al's office waiting for their "sentencing," and, gradually, the tension that had usually gripped the building eased. A respectful environment came to exist for the first time in many years. In the beginning, there were many discussions about RTP and whether or not the process would work. Staff still wanted to know what was going to happen to the students who misbehaved. Some wanted to know what operational procedures we had in place to deal with the frequent flyers, and they especially wanted to know how many RTC visits would dictate a trip home. (It was difficult to get away from stimulus-response practice!) Many of the staff looked at the process as simply a compliance program in which students told the teachers what the teachers wanted to hear.

Because we did not fully understand plan making, we

allowed students to write "cookie-cutter" plans, to make weak commitments about following the rules, and to negotiate their plans inadequately with their teachers. Probably the biggest question teachers had (and still have today) concerned students missing valuable class time. If students are in the RTC because they have been disruptive in class, how are they going to get instruction? The teachers had a difficult time understanding the RTC as a place for learning—namely, for learning social skills. If a student is disruptive in class, that student is not learning the material. However, while the disrupting student is in RTC, the other students in the class have the opportunity to learn without disruption, and the classroom environment is maintained. While Al was piloting the process, the other school administrators were introducing RTP to their staffs and trying to answer questions raised by both teachers and parents. Shortly after the middle school began using the process, the other buildings started using RTP.

When we started with RTP, the traditional perceptions of building principals were deeply entrenched in both our schools. Those perceptions hindered our attempts to fulfill our roles as RTP administrators. RTP administrators must drive the process, and we needed to fight the traditional stereotypes while working to establish RTP in our schools. We were introducing a process in which students are allowed to decide how they want things to be while respecting the rights of others, and in which the adults support the students' decisions. Contrast that with the traditional view that administrators are supposed to be "in control of" all aspects of the school environment, including people. To let students decide how *they* want things to be is in direct conflict with all the college classes designed to teach educators how to "manage" buildings and classrooms. Both of us realized quickly that *using RTP would be a major paradigm shift, and not only would create conflict in many students in our schools, but also would create conflict for a number of the adults, including parents, administrators, and teachers.*

For some of our students, accepting responsibility for themselves created enormous conflicts. And teachers who, before, had been responsible for making students behave were being asked to stop trying to control students and instead allow them to decide how they wanted to be. Administrators, who were responsible for bringing RTP to the district, experienced conflict because of growing community concerns about the feasibility of success with RTP at Evart Public Schools. In the initial implementation of RTP in our schools, the waters were tested many times. As students went home and parents got upset, both of us had to reflect on what we were doing. Parents of frequent flyers expressed their displeasure with the process, because their children were going home on a regular basis. Those parents saw RTP as punitive and believed their children were singled out for trivial reasons. One parent was livid when his student went home for tapping his pencil while he was in the RTC. He failed to see that his son had disrupted for the fourth time that day, twice in the classroom, and twice in the RTC.

There were moments of real despair as those around us questioned our sanity and integrity for even *thinking* about bringing RTP to our district. Teachers questioned whether RTP was working, because, in the beginning, many students went home from the RTC. Community members called school board members to complain about the process and were skeptical about students being responsible for themselves—they said they wondered what we were paying school employees to do. During that time in our RTP history, there were many sleepless nights, many conferences with students and parents, and many questions raised by our teaching staffs and community. The culmination of those conflicts left us alone with our thoughts and the burning questions that needed to be answered. We were in different buildings, but issues such as formulating appropriate operational procedures, dealing with student plans, handling frequent flyers, and establishing the intent of RTP were strikingly similar for both of us. As we worked

through these issues, answers slowly ?
By reading material about RTP and ?
calls and e-mails to Ed Ford, we were ab??
answers and then ask more questions to get ot??
ing about what we were doing. The more we worked ?
issues and problems, the clearer the path seemed to appear, and the fewer additional questions arose. We have
talked about the beginning of our RTP experience many
times, but only recently have we realized that during that
stressful time, *we were going through reorganization—*
reorganization that continues to this day! Just as Karen
reorganized as she sat for a month in the RTC, we too were
struggling with conflicts we experienced as a result of
implementing RTP in our schools, and the teachers in our
buildings provided us with many additional examples of
reorganization as they struggled with the differences between RTP and the existing student discipline models they
had lived with and believed in for years.

Most teachers' conflicts were due to having been trained
to handle discipline in the classroom by using cause-effect
and stimulus-response methodologies. They had tried
proximity techniques, various forms of assertive discipline
techniques, and other types of behavior modification methods to control their students. The ineffectiveness of such
techniques was a source of frustration for those wanting to
be perceived as "good" teachers. We suspect that millions
of teachers in this country are "burned out" by trying to
control students' behavior. As Ed has often suggested,
"Never try to change that over which you have no control."

Before RTP, most teachers at Evart Middle School and
Evart High School were quite frustrated and literally prayed
to make it through each day. Many had basically given up
hope of ever returning to their first love, teaching, because
of the incessant demands of student discipline. Then along
came RTP and PCT, telling educators that everything they
had been taught about human behavior and controlling
that behavior in their rooms is wrong. Imagine being those
frustrated teachers, sitting in an auditorium, listening to Ed

and George Venetis propose a new, completely differ-
way of dealing with students. Imagine the conflict and
ısbelief the teachers experience as they realize that perhaps they have been wrong for years—or thinking that Ed
and George are clueless about what goes on in real-world
education. Imagine the responses displayed by school staff,
who have arrived at various positions with regard to discipline issues through a diversity of experiences. How would
an administrator even *begin* to handle their questions,
doubts, and emotions?

Consider Mary, who has recently graduated from college
and is ready to change the world, "one student at a time."
She is armed with her bag of tricks and methods taught by
respected scholars at a university, and she feels confident
that she is prepared to handle the real world of teaching.
Like most new teachers, Mary experiences a honeymoon
period and continues to feel as if she is at the top of her
game. After a while, the honeymoon ends, and Mary starts
feeling frustrated with her students; she reaches into her
bag of tricks to see if they actually *do* work. They work
for a while, but soon Mary realizes that for each trick she
tries, the students have an answer. Frustrated, she turns to
others for help and is disappointed by the responses she
hears. Increasingly desperate, she tries even the most out-
rageous tricks, because, she thinks, *something* must work.

Then Mary is hired to teach in a school that uses the
Responsible Thinking Process. She reads some of what she
is given by her administrator, but she is confident that her
previous training has adequately prepared her for her new
job. However, her frustration returns. Finally, as a last re-
sort, she makes an appointment to see her principal and
ask for help. Mary is disillusioned and afraid as she prepares
for the meeting. She has developed strong feelings of being
inadequate. She feels defeated and hopeless but is willing
to try anything to salvage some semblance of the vision she
once had of teaching.

Mary arrives at the principal's office and hopes that she
can hold off her tears. But as she begins to speak, the tears

begin flowing freely. The principal sees Mary's signs of conflict and realizes that she should be given an opportunity to reorganize her thoughts. Mary describes a technique she used when her class was out of control just recently. She was told in a college class that when the students in her room are out of control, she should tell them to put their heads down on their desks until they are all quiet and "in control." Unfortunately, that technique had failed miserably, and many of the students who had not been disrupting seemed to feel disrespected. Furthermore, the students knew how RTP is supposed to work and soon realized that Mary wasn't using the process. (A common complaint of students in RTP schools is that some teachers don't use the process consistently, or at all.) The principal asks Mary how she would feel if he used the heads-down technique at a staff meeting when the teachers were talking. Mary continues to cry as the questions keep coming from the principal. (We have found the RTP questioning techniques work as well with teachers as they do with students.)

Mary's internal struggling is reorganization at work. The skilled RTP administrator recognizes the signs of reorganization and now tries to act as a *means of control* for Mary, rather than as a disturbance for her, as she reorganizes her thoughts. During this difficult time, the administrator needs to be compassionate and express confidence that Mary can resolve her conflicts, asking pertinent questions to determine where Mary is in terms of her understanding of RTP. For example, he might ask: "What would you like your classroom to look like?" "What do you consider a disruption in your classroom?" "How do students know when they have disrupted?" "How many times should a student be allowed to disrupt?" He might ask how she takes care of classroom disruptions; after she describes her techniques, he could then ask: "Do you think they are working?" If she doesn't think the techniques are working, he could ask: "What do you think might work?" Based on Mary's responses, the questioning would give him a glimpse of Mary's world. As administrators in an RTP school, we know *the secret to working with teachers who are reorganizing is to use the concepts inherent within RTP and PCT while they are in conflict.* By using the process, we are not acting as a disturbance, and we are allowing the teachers the time they need for internal reflection. We become means of control for the teachers. As we work with them, relationships develop that allow us to help them resolve their conflicts while showing them respect. As the teachers then experience some success from the plans they have developed, they act according to the internal standards they create as a result of reorganization. The conflicts are handled in a respectful manner, and meaningful dialogue establishes guidelines for future problem-solving adventures.

As we implemented RTP, reorganization also occurred within veteran teachers who felt that their cause-effect techniques had worked well in the past and thus saw no real reasons to change. Historically, veteran teachers have used administrators as buffers from angry students and parents, while refusing to accept any responsibility for overall student discipline. Students were sent to the principal to cure any disruptive behavior, ranging from not having a pencil to fighting in school. The administrator was supposed to solve all the problems, and if the problems weren't solved to the teachers' satisfaction, the teachers felt unsupported; the teachers wanted and expected something to happen to the students to curb their disruptions. When RTP was introduced into our schools, some teachers had a difficult time shifting from a traditional discipline system to RTP. Using RTP, disruptive students went to the RTC to work on plans to solve their problems. Some teachers still wanted to know what was going to happen to the students because of their behavior. Teachers wanted to rely on the cause-effect way of thinking to deal with student disruptions, even when they were supposed to be using RTP as the model.

As administrators, we needed to help our teachers look internally and decide how they wanted things to be, while maintaining the integrity of RTP. We have used several methods to help facilitate the reorganization and education of our staff with regard to RTP's principles. One of these methods is staff discussion of the process. We encourage teachers to talk openly about what they have experienced and tried in their classrooms. Teachers are encouraged to bring up specific situations, such as a student shouting out in class. As a group, we discuss and role play the situations, making suggestions about the process in general, as well as specific classroom management techniques that might help prevent these situations from occurring. While discussing the situations, we remind teachers that we are trying to maintain the integrity of the learning environment.

Another method we use is to go through *Book One* and *Book Two* of *Discipline for Home and School*, working on jigsaw activities during teacher meetings. The jigsaw is a cooperative learning strategy where the teachers are placed in groups and required to become resident experts for one chapter of the books. Then they move into new groups and teach the material to their colleagues. Our teachers have responded enthusiastically to jigsaw activities, realizing that they all can contribute to the overall success and understanding of RTP in our schools.

To further their understanding of RTP and its place in an educational setting, we have had dialogues comparing RTP procedures to the operational procedures used in other classroom situations where students might experience difficulties (such as math or language arts); the emphasis is on how we can help students with their conflicts, rather than punish them. If students are experiencing difficulty in math, for example, educators spend additional time tutoring them to make sure they understood the concepts. Any good teacher develops ways to present information and then check student understanding. Good teachers do pretty much whatever is needed to make sure students learn academic material. A student is not punished for struggling in math; instead, help is offered. If a student is struggling with behavior, help should also be offered.

We have gradually learned to recognize and facilitate the reorganization we *all* experience as conflicted living control systems. This goes far beyond our initial perceptions regarding RTP and PCT. In fact, we remember, early on, telling ourselves that the chapters on PCT in *Book One* are not all that important as long as we understood how the process is supposed to work. How wrong we were! We now know that RTP and PCT *cannot* be separated, because this process goes *beyond* discipline in schools.

RTP has allowed us to see and experience how living control systems work, and how they should be treated. For both of us, RTP and PCT have changed our lives as individuals, husbands, fathers, and educators. We are forever grateful to Ed Ford for working with us as we have continued to struggle to understand the deeper meanings of this process. We have come a long way, and the journey has been awesome! We are looking forward to continuing our work with RTP and PCT, and we realize our odyssey has just begun.

Chapter 5
RTP and Me

George T. Venetis
Retired School Administrator
RTP Trainer and Evaluator

I was an elementary teacher for twenty years and a school administrator for nine years, and I've been an RTP trainer and evaluator for the last four years. I'll never forget the time, about ten years ago, when we first brought in Ed Ford to implement the Responsible Thinking Process. I was assistant principal at Clarendon School in the Osborn Elementary School District in an urban area in Phoenix. We had 450 fourth, fifth, and sixth grade students. I remember what I initially found appealing about RTP. I learned that RTP is based on perceptual control theory, which shows that we are all designed as living control systems and, as such, are always controlling for what we want—in other words, it isn't the environment that controls us. We are all accountable and responsible for what we control, but we can't be held accountable and responsible for that which we don't control, i.e., student behavior. Each student is accountable and responsible for what he does. When I heard that I would be held accountable and responsible only for that which I control (such as following RTP), and that my role in implementing the process would be clearly defined, I thought, "It's about time!"

I now had a process based on solid principles that I could easily apply in all situations when interacting with others. RTP could be used to deal effectively with all disciplinary issues. I found that the more I used this process, the more proficient I became in dealing with others. For example, I remember the time Ed Ford joined me on the school playground for recess duty, and, right in front of us, one boy hit another boy in the face. After separating them, I asked the boy who had done the punching what he just did. He replied, "Nothing." I then told him that I saw him hit the other boy in the face and asked whether he thought I was going to believe my eyes or what he just told me. There was a short pause, and then he said, "Well, I didn't hit him that hard." We then proceeded to my office, where we continued the process.

Before implementing RTP, I would have handled that situation much differently. I would have gotten right up in the student's face, trying to use fear and intimidation to make sure he would never hit another student again. I would have suspended him from school as a punishment for what he did, hoping that would change his behavior. And when that failed to work, I would have increased the number of days of his suspension. I would have done everything I could to try to force him to change that over which I had no control: his behavior. But with RTP, instead of yelling and telling, I calmly ask questions—questions that help students think about, reflect on, and compare what they are doing with the rules and standards of the school; questions that move students from the behavioral level, where problems are never solved, to a higher level, where rules and standards can act as guides to help them decide how they want to be.

Reflecting on my years as a school principal, I recall the time two of our toughest sixth grade girls came to me requesting the use of my office. They had gotten into a disagreement during their lunch recess, and, instead of fighting, they went into the girls' restroom to try to talk it out. There was one problem, however: their so-called friends followed them into the restroom and kept trying to get them to fight. So the girls wanted to use my office to try to resolve their conflict. I remember watching in amazement as these two girls, who had been in numerous physical fights with other students, sat in my office and talked through their differences. When they were finished, they stood up and hugged each other, then turned and thanked me. As they walked away, I thought of all the times I had dealt with these girls when they had gotten into fights with other students, and all the conflict resolutions through negotiations I helped them through after each fight. I was beginning to wonder if they were learning anything from those experiences. I can't help but think that if I hadn't used RTP, if I hadn't had the patience to continue to work with the girls, and if I hadn't continued to provide them with the experience of resolving their conflicts through negotiating, they would never have learned to work together to resolve their problems.

There was another time when students came to my office during their recess to make a request. This time it was three fifth grade boys who came to ask if they could spend the remainder of the school day in the Responsible Thinking Classroom. I saw this as an unusual request since most students work hard to stay out of the RTC. When I asked them for the reason they wanted to go to the RTC, they informed me that they had a substitute teacher who was doing a lot of yelling at the class, and they were afraid they would eventually get angry and do something that would get them into trouble. They wanted to go to the RTC, where they knew they would be treated nicely, just like their regular teacher treated them. I asked them how they planned to make up the work they would miss by not being in class. They said their regular teacher had provided packets of work for them to do whenever they had a substitute teacher, and they would work on those packets in the RTC. I then asked them what would happen if they disrupted in the RTC. They said they would be sent home, but I didn't have to worry about that, because they wouldn't disrupt there. I then escorted the three boys to our RTC, where I explained to the RTC teacher what was going on. Before returning to my office, I stopped by the boys' regular classroom to talk to the substitute teacher. As I approached the room, I could hear her yelling at the class. I told the teacher about the three students who would be spending the rest of the day in the RTC, and I also reviewed RTP with her. This was another reminder to me of how students, just like everyone else, like to be treated with respect, and that once they experience being treated that way through RTP, they come to expect it from everyone. In fact, once we started using RTP, the complaints I heard most often from students were about teachers not asking the RTP questions and teachers who would ask the questions to some students but not others.

As Ed and I travel around the country conducting RTP trainings, one question we often hear is "What about the students for whom nothing seems to work? Can RTP help those students?" This always brings to mind one of our sixth grade students who was a "frequent flyer," one of those students who spend a lot of time in the Responsible Thinking Classroom. Making matters worse, each time the student got into trouble, his mother would come to school and blame us for the problems her son was having. This being the case, a few of our staff members began to wonder whether it might be better for both the student and the school if he were suspended for the remainder of the school year. As we continued to conduct RTP Intervention Team meetings concerning this young man, and as we continued to work with him and spend quality time with him, I began to notice that his visits to the RTC were becoming less frequent. In fact, by the end of the school year, not only was he disrupting less, he also started to improve academically. Two years after this student left our school, his mother came back to tell us that her son was not only an honor student at his present school, but also elected eighth grade class president. With tears in her eyes, she told us that she just had to stop by to thank us for putting up with her all those years, and for never giving up on her son. Wow! Isn't that what it is really all about? Following the process and never giving up on a student, no matter how long it takes for him to struggle through and reorganize—that's what can help "frequent flyers" learn to think more responsibly.

And that's what can help all students achieve long-term changes. I remember the time when Ed and I entered the RTC at Evart High School in Michigan, and I immediately noticed a young man sitting in the back of the room who seemed a little upset. When I asked him how things were going, he didn't hesitate to let me know in no uncertain terms that he really wasn't very happy. And when I asked him what was wrong, he replied, "This school sucks!" "Oh, really?" I said. "What makes this school suck?" To which he responded, "At this school, when you get into trouble, you have to answer a bunch of dumb questions and think about what you're doing. And if you continue to disrupt, you have to go to this dumb room and complete a plan, and you have to meet with the RTC teacher to go over your plan before you can return to class to review your plan with your teacher. You really have to do a lot of work. I want to go back to my old school in Florida." "Why do you want to go back to your other school?" I asked. He answered, "Because, at my other school, when you got into trouble all you had to do was go to detention or get suspended from school. No big deal. You just served your time, and then you got to go back to class. It was easy. You didn't have to work at it." I then asked, "What did you learn from that experience at your other school?" "Nothing," he replied. "It was just easier."

That really says it all, doesn't it?

Finally, concluding my reflections on the past thirty-three years, I remember a letter from a teacher who described the internal struggle she went through while using the process. She wrote, "The questions I'm required to ask students who are making poor choices are difficult for me, because I, too, do not take responsibility for my actions. I have spent a lifetime blaming what I do on other people, rather than realizing that I, and I alone, chose to do or say certain things. While others' actions and words certainly affect my thinking, I have had to learn and accept responsibility for my own decisions and actions and the consequences of those. . . . As I read back over this paragraph, I realize that anyone who is honest with themselves could have written this." (See *Discipline For Home and School, Book Two*, page 12.)

This is really what RTP is all about: *being honest with ourselves*. It's all about, as Ed always says, looking within ourselves and deciding how we each want to be. That's where the real conflicts occur, within ourselves. At one of the RTP trainings, a teacher asked about students who repeatedly made her angry and upset. As we took this teacher through the PCT model to help explain what was happening between her and the students who she said made her angry, the teacher suddenly blurted out, "The conflict is really within me. It's not the student who's making feel me this way." This is the kind of revelation I hear over and over again from educators around the world as they continue to use RTP, and as they begin to understand the principles that guide this process.

As you continue to use RTP, do you take time to look within yourself to determine how you want to be? Do you look within yourself as you deal with various conflicts and problems, and do you allow others to do the same? This is what RTP is all about.

Chapter 6
Perceptual Control Theory
on Personal Change

William T. Powers
Perceptual Control Theorist
Durango, Colorado

One of the main techniques of RTP is asking questions. Ed Ford explains that asking questions, rather than giving orders or demanding action, leads students to think. But why should asking questions have that effect? What does it make them think? And why should thinking alter anything? A simple experiment might suggest some answers.

Right now you're reading words in a book. Of course before I mentioned that, you were already reading, but I doubt that you were you saying to yourself, "Hey, look, I'm reading words in a book!" You weren't observing the fact that you were reading; you were just doing it. Somehow when I mentioned the reading, something shifted in your consciousness, so that not only the words on the page occupied your attention, but your own process of reading came into mental view. A similar effect happens when I call your attention to something that is obviously being sensed, but that you're not conscious of at the moment, such as the pressure from the seat you're sitting in. Just mention such a thing, and it pops into your conscious world. Where was it before? Your sensory nerves were most probably working the same way before and after. The difference is in where your attention was focused.

There is another related phenomenon. Right now, in the foreground of your attention, is this sentence and the meanings it is bringing forth in your mind. But as you go on reading, there is another layer of thoughts, or feelings, or attitudes—call them thoughts. They are thoughts about what you are reading. I hope your thought is something like "This is interesting," but even if it's "This is garbage," you're having *a background thought about what is going on in the foreground.*

I sometimes introduce these ideas to an audience. First I ask the audience members to focus on some thoughts that they're having right at the moment. Then I ask each of them to experience that thought while he or she detects a background thought about the foreground thought. And finally, I ask all those who found a background thought in their minds to raise their hands. Usually, most of the people will raise their hands, leaving a handful of people looking uncomfortable or dismayed. Then I ask, "Now, will all the people who are thinking something like 'Gee, this is working for everyone but me' raise their hands?" That usually gets the rest of the hands in the air, not to mention a laugh as the left-out people realize what their background thought actually was.

I think this works with everyone. But not everyone immediately recognizes what the background thought is. Sometimes it's not a normal thought, but just a feeling or attitude. You don't have to think the words "It's working for everyone but me" to feel a little discouraged and left out. That discouragement and left-out feeling is about *what is going on in the foreground.* That's what I call a background thought. This is a pretty reliable phenomenon. It's hard to imagine drawing a complete blank when you look for a background thought, especially when you realize that you're thinking, "I'm drawing a complete blank."

This hasn't told you why questioning works or what it does, but we're getting there. Clearly, asking a question like "What are you doing?" can call a person's attention to the fact that he is doing something (like running in the hall), so now he is no longer just doing it while attending to something else (like hoping he won't be late for class), but is aware of the process of doing it—of, in fact, intending to do it.

A basic principle of PCT is that higher-order control systems in the brain act by setting the goals that lower-order control systems carry out. That's a theoretical model of the brain, but we can see that it must have something to do with what we're talking about here—first, being able to focus attention on one control process (a perception and an action, that is), and second, being able to extend attention to another control process at the same time, so for a while you are aware of two things at the same time.

What PCT tells us is that these two processes are not independent, like chewing gum and walking across the room are. They are related to each other. The background thought is associated with a control process that is at a higher level than the control process associated with the foreground thought. I use the loose term "associated" because I don't know exactly what the relationship is. When you are asked "What are you doing?" this little jogging of your attention makes you aware of two levels of control at the same time: the immediate intention or effect of what you're doing (of which you were already aware) and the higher-level intention or effect you are getting by exerting the lower-level control (which was probably not in your conscious attention).

There's one more effect, and this brings us to the point. When Johnny is running in the hall to avoid being late to class, his attention is on his immediate problem: being late. In fact, he is so wrapped up in trying not to be late that he is not even aware of trying not to be late—he's just running, and being late. He is experiencing the world consciously as if he *is* that control process, looking through its eyes at the clock and the distance to the classroom, and acting with its means of acting, which is telling the control systems that work his legs to produce running.

When the hall monitor says, "Johnny, what are you doing?" it is quite likely that Johnny will stop and say something like "Trying not to be late for class." Asking a person what he or she is doing requires that the person look first to see what he or she is doing. It's like asking, "What color is that stone you're standing on?" To see what color the stone is, you have to look at the place where it is, and *you have to stand somewhere else* because your foot is on the stone. You can't stand on the stone and describe it at the same time. So asking a person "What are you doing?" requires that the person move to a *different* point of view to describe what he or she is trying to do. And because of the hierarchical arrangement of control systems in the brain, the person must shift to a *higher-level* point of view in order to answer the question. The effect of this shift is often startling, for shifting to a higher point of view can alter a person's whole state of thinking and feeling. It's like radically changing the subject, including both what you're thinking and what you're feeling about it. The questioner doesn't do anything wonderful or mysterious, or offer any insights or solutions to problems, yet the effect on the other person can be profound.

Why should simply changing the focus of attention have such an effect? The answer requires that we talk about *reorganization*. This is proposed in PCT as what a person does when all else fails—when nothing is helping to solve a problem. It's also been called "trial-and-error learning." As that term implies, there's a component of randomness in it.

When problems persist, a human being falls back on this basic process, which operates from the very beginning of childhood. It has to start operating early, because it has to work before one has learned anything else. It *creates* the other methods we use to solve problems, by reorganizing the way the brain perceives and solves problems. Creating some organization out of almost none is one result of reorganization.

When we are having problems controlling our worlds, these problems can begin to affect us at deep levels, the way hunger and lack of air and pain and fear affect us. Even without knowing in detail how this happens, we can guess that feeling bad in very basic ways leads to random changes in the brain—literally physical changes in how things are connected, I think. Why "random" changes? Simply because none of the systematic ways of changing things known to the person have worked. Random is all that is left.

But won't random changes have effects for the worse at least as often as effects for the better? Yes. However, random changes can be used in a way that increases the chances of good effects and reduces the chances of bad effects. It works like this. Suppose some little change happens in your brain, by a mechanism we can't explain at present, and as a result you start behaving differently. Behaving differently means that you interact with your world differently—you might see new things to control, or find new ways to control familiar things, or decide you don't need to control a particular thing any more. Most anything can result from such random reorganization. Because you're behaving a little differently, you're moving through life in a slightly different direction. If you're going in a new direction and it seems to make your bad feelings worse, what do you do? You might say "undo the change," but that would mean having memories and knowing the concept of "opposite" and a lot of other things you can't do until after you've learned them. Reorganization has to work before you've learned anything. So what do you do? *You make another change, at random, and take off in a new direction.* Because there is no guarantee that the new direction will be any better than the previous one, the result of the change might be to feel even worse than before. So you change again. And again, and again, until eventually it might happen that you change in a way that produces a kind of behavior making your bad feelings a little less bad. So now what do you do? You don't reorganize again right away. You leave things alone for a bit and keep on in the same direction, as long as you keep feeling better and better. But this might eventually lead to feeling a little worse again, and if it does, you change, and change, and change again, until the trend is once again toward feeling better.

What will be the ultimate end of such a reorganization process? If you change and feel worse, you don't go far that way, but try another change almost immediately. If you feel better, you go on that way for a while before reorganizing again. *The net result is that you will go a lot farther, on the average, in the directions that make you feel better than the other directions that make you feel worse.* If there is some way of behaving (within the range of behaviors that can be brought about this way) that will make the bad feelings go away entirely, you (or this reorganizing system we're talking about) are likely to get there eventually. And then you will stop reorganizing.

When you stop *re*organizing, you are then *organized* in a particular way: the way that produces behavior keeping the bad feelings from occurring. Since the bad feelings are gone, the changes have stopped; since the changes have stopped, your organization will stay as it is. You have learned a behavior that keeps you from having those very basic bad feelings. The "very basic bad feelings" might seem mysterious, but they aren't. They're just built-in feelings that tell you something is wrong with your basic life-support systems. They're the sorts of things you feel when you have emotions such as anger or fear, or feelings of being hungry, sick, exhausted, or short of breath. A baby will reject a bottle at first, but if hungry will reorganize until it accepts the bottle and makes the hunger go away and stops the reorganizing. A child suffering from a lack of love will reorganize until he or she learns to do something that makes that bad feeling go away—like joining a gang, if that's all that's available—and then the reorganizing stops.

Reorganization can remove the bad feeling without the reorganizing person understanding anything at all about what is going on. This is precisely what is needed when no existing skills are working, or when you don't have any skills yet. This is what allows the reorganizing process to work when all else has failed.

One thing that hasn't been mentioned yet is *what* gets reorganized, other than "the brain." A hidden problem here is that when you reorganize, the way your brain works changes, and if it is already doing something as well as possible for you, like playing the piano, you don't want to start reorganizing that skill at random, which can only make it worse. All athletes know that you have to stop practicing when you reach a peak of skill, or the skill will start to degrade. And they know without even thinking about it that if the problem is with your girlfriend, you don't want to reorganize your high-jumping, but your way of behaving with your girlfriend. To reorganize something that is already very well organized is to *dis*organize it. *What is it that directs reorganiztion to the part of your brain that needs it and not to the parts that don't need it?*

Suppose that the focus of our attention also serves to focus reorganization, assuming that the conditions are such as to cause reorganization to start. We all know that a physical problem, such as a sore toe, can grab our attention very effectively. So can psychological problems, like embarrassment. And most of the time, when we become aware of a problem and focus on it, the problem eventually is solved. Reorganization apparently *automatically* happens where it is needed, and not where it would make things worse, and it stops when we have changed in ways that lead to feeling good again. Attention can quickly focus on the part of our experience where a problem is happening; this apparently drags the focus of reorganization to the corresponding part of the brain, and random changes alter the connections in that part of the brain.

Of course, given the randomness in reorganization, we might be unlucky. We might get stuck in a situation where little changes in *any* direction make us feel worse, and only a big change, or a change in some unexpected direction, can make a substantial change for the better. And, worst of all, attention might get dragged to a problem that is really being caused by something else in the brain, so we could reorganize continuously where attention is focused without affecting the problem at all. Thus, it is necessary to be patient with those going through the reorganization process. And it is possible that the process might never end for some individuals. All you can do is continue to work with them while you are able.

A student entering the RTC is likely to be emotionally upset, embarrassed, feeling badly or unfairly treated, and/or apprehensive about what might happen next. In short, the child is most probably in an internal state that is likely to produce reorganization. Probably the most important thing to understand about reorganization is that it is automatic, not under conscious control. And if, as proposed in PCT, the changes it induces are random or at least unsystematic, nothing can be done to steer the process toward any particular outcome. Reorganizing might take a considerable time to produce something that seems better to the child or to anyone else. So, the process of reorganizing has to be left to work by itself—the child has to be left alone in peace and quiet to go through the immediate pain and turmoil and find, within, the willingness to seek help.

However, others can help reorganization focus in a useful way by asking a few questions and by imparting an important piece of information. The questions are designed to get the child to examine how he or she is feeling about being sent to the RTC. As we have seen, the effect of this is to get the child to look at the feelings from a different point of view rather than identifying with them and acting out the thoughts that go with them. Pointed or leading questions (such as "Do you have the least idea why you're here *again*?") are counterproductive. All that is needed is to direct attention to inner states of feeling and thought: "Are you bothered about being here? In what ways? What do you think about it? Would you like some time to figure out what happened before we talk?" Once you get the idea of simply directing attention to the foreground feelings and thoughts from some other point of view, such questions are not hard to devise.

And the important piece of information is this: "It's OK to feel upset. That's how people feel when they're having a problem and haven't figured out the solution yet. While you're feeling this way, all sorts of ideas and thoughts will come up, which is how you get new ideas. When you get an idea that looks good, you might feel a lot better. Take your time, and let me know when you want to talk about it."

This is not a rote speech to be delivered from memory, but an idea to get across to the child in the RTC teacher's own words and style. Being upset—reorganizing—is not a sign of losing a battle or being proven wrong, and it doesn't mean that something is the matter with you. It's just the result of getting into a bad situation and not seeing a way out of it yet. Being left alone doesn't mean you're being abandoned. If you just go through this bad period, your mind will bring up new answers, some bad and some good, and pretty soon you will see something you might actually do that's effective. All human beings work this way: the teacher in your classroom does, I do, and you do, too.

Chapter 7
Do *You* Take RTP Seriously?

Greg Williams
Editor of RTP and PCT Books
Gravel Switch, Kentucky

In Chapter 1, Ed Ford describes how, with RTP, chronically disrupting students can learn to become more responsible. That chapter and Appendix 1 explain the "turn around" in these students' lives from the standpoint of how humans are constructed to behave as modeled by perceptual control theory (PCT), which is the foundation upon which RTP is built. In this chapter, rather than focusing on what is going on within these students, I want to explore *what should be going on within educators*, especially Responsible Thinking Classroom (RTC) teachers, who are trying to facilitate the students' "turn around."

Ed shows that, when starting on the path to becoming more responsible, chronically disrupting students initially need some time to struggle with their priorities *within themselves*. Then, as the students begin to build the self-confidence necessary to turn around their lives, assistance from educators is appropriate *as requested by the students*. Effective support for the students requires respecting their own efforts to turn their lives around, rather than attempting to judge those efforts or to dictate alterations in them. RTP procedures (such as the questions) were designed in accordance with PCT to prevent such attempts to control students.

But just following the procedures isn't enough. It is certainly possible to go through the motions, applying RTP procedures "by rote," so to speak, without *believing in* the principles (based on PCT models of human behavior) underlying those procedures. And just going through the motions is *not* what RTP is all about. The chronically disrupting student who dutifully writes yet another plan and successfully negotiates once again with his teacher in the class in which he disrupted, only to find himself back in the RTC the next day, might be following the procedures—but in a quite superficial way. *He's not taking RTP seriously.* He hasn't gone through the struggle discussed by Ed and made a *genuine* commitment to becoming more responsible.

Students aren't the only ones who can treat RTP superficially. Unfortunately, there are also educators in some RTP schools who don't take RTP seriously, even though they might appear to follow the procedures (at least to a degree) each day. The educators running the "terribly wrong" RTC described by Ed Ford in his chapter obviously showed little concern for the PCT-based reasons behind the procedures, since they altered the procedures in various ways apparently contrary to PCT ideas. But the superficial, uncommitted application of RTP by educators isn't necessarily so obvious. A classroom teacher could always ask the questions at the appropriate times, with the correct phrasing, and in the right order—and yet with a vengeful tone of voice. An RTC teacher could fulfill all of his recordkeeping needs "to the letter"—and still answer students' questions with cold and superficial answers. A principal could carefully monitor statistics on referrals and other data showing RTP's effectiveness in her school—and still refuse to meet regularly with teachers who need help with the process. In each of these cases, the educator might be having success with RTP in the short-term, but Ed Ford and RTP administrators of accredited schools know from experience with such situations that there will be difficulties in the longer term—when students want to "get back at" that classroom teacher, or when students come to see that RTC teacher as not really caring much about them, or when teachers having difficulty with RTP give up entirely on trying to use it in that principal's school.

The chances of long-term success with RTP are *much*

enhanced if the principles on which it is based are *internalized* by the educators using the process. This is *completely* different from applying RTP procedures *without believing in them*—without, that is, taking them *seriously*. And, at least for educators who have previously internalized and taken seriously principles (such as stimulus-response psychology and reward-and-punishment discipline schemes) that *contradict* principles derived from PCT, internalization of PCT principles can be expected to require an internal struggle like that experienced by chronically disrupting students when they start out on the path to becoming more responsible.

The PCT principles that need to be internalized for long-term successful application of RTP aren't based on complicated details of PCT models of human behavior, but instead on some rather simple general features of those models. The principles appear when the models are viewed from a distance, as it were. Here, I'll suggest three primary principles that can be understood without studying PCT in depth; if you want to learn more about the details of PCT models, I suggest beginning with *Making Sense of Behavior* by William T. Powers.

Perhaps the most obvious general feature of PCT models of human behavior is the basically similar organizational structure postulated for every individual. PCT says that *each* of us is organized to behave so as to try, at any given time, to get what each of us *individually* wants at that time. *All* people behave *solely* for only *one* kind of reason (namely, to try to get what they individually want at a given time), and *nobody* behaves for *other* kinds of reasons. In particular, nobody behaves a certain way for *no* reasons at all, and nobody behaves a certain way because somebody (or something) else "made" them behave that way. Thus, we arrive at

Principle 1: *All people are personally responsible for their own behavior.*

To internalize this principle means to incorporate it into one's personality so that it becomes an ongoing functional guideline in daily life. Believing that each person (including oneself) is *solely* responsible for his or her own behavior flatly contradicts various other principles, such as the belief that some object (such as money) in a person's environment, or another person, or perhaps even a "demon" is responsible for his or her behavior. Just like chronically disruptive students who haven't internalized this principle of personal responsibility, educators who believe that the students' parents (or peers, or television shows, or anything else besides the students themselves) are responsible for their disruptive behaviors *are not taking RTP seriously*. Neither the students nor the educators can be expected to be strongly committed to a process in tune with a principle that they aren't "living" on a daily basis.

Another general feature of PCT models of human behavior is their lack of "transparency." Most of a person's behavioral organization lies *within* that person, *unseen* by other persons. So it is often not apparent why someone behaves in a particular way—in other words, thinking back to the derivation of Principle 1, it is often not apparent what someone is trying to accomplish. If you simply try to *guess* what another person wants, you might be *completely* wrong—did Bobby whisper in class because he wanted to annoy the teacher, or because he wanted to make sure he heard correctly what the teacher had been saying—or because he wanted something else entirely? What you *can* observe *as a result of* another's behavioral organization is how he or she *acts*, and you might be tempted to make inferences about the person's internal organization based on such observations. But even if you *ask* a person what they actually want, and you receive an answer, *understanding* much about the person's internal organization is iffy, because you have only highly *indirect* access (*through* the person) to that organization. The only one with *direct* access is the person to whom the organization belongs, making an exploration of that organization very difficult from the "outside." This leads to

> Principle 2: *It is difficult to explore another's behavioral organization; it is easier to explore one's own organization.*

Internalizing this principle means coming to believe that it is unlikely that you have others "all figured out" so that they can be "read like a book." It also means coming to believe that you shouldn't spend a lot of time and effort trying to "analyze" others' behavioral organizations, since it is likely to be much more efficient to facilitate their *own* explorations of themselves. To help educators avoid trying to analyze the internal structures of students, RTP emphasizes questioning that tends to encourage exploration of those structures by the students themselves (particularly with regard to setting priorities in accord with the rules of where the students are: "What are you doing?"). But educators who don't take RTP seriously—who haven't internalized Principle 2—might be tempted to ask *leading* questions, such as "If you don't want to end up in the RTC again tomorrow, what should you change in your plan?" (threatening retribution) or "Why don't you just shut up in class?" (ignoring the complexity of the student's behavioral organization).

Taken together, the belief in personal responsibility, from Principle 1, and the difficulty of understanding anyone else's behavioral organization, from Principle 2, suggest

> Principle 3: *To genuinely help others, facilitate their* own *ability to get what they want, instead of trying to provide them with what you* think *they want or what* you *want* them to want.

This principle might remind you of the Golden Rule, "Do unto others as you would have them do unto you," but it includes some qualifications not explicitly stated in the

Golden Rule, making it more closely related to what long-time PCT student Dag Forssell has called the Diamond Rule: "Do unto others as they would have you do unto them." The point here is that "help" is not necessarily helpful if you offer it so that someone can get *what you want the person to get* instead of *what the person wants to get.* You don't have the behavioral organization required to satisfy others' wants *directly* for them—your behavioral organization is solely your own, not anyone else's (Principle 1). Nor are you well-equipped to analyze others' behavioral organizations so as to satisfy their wants *indirectly* (Principle 2). So trying to substitute for someone else's behavioral organization is a risky business at best!

This belief flatly contradicts various other principles, such as the authoritarian belief that it is possible to "know better than they do what's good for" others. As discussed above, because there is no direct access to the internal parts of another's behavioral organization, *guessing* or *assuming* a certain structure for that organization will likely be incorrect. And so will *prescribing* a certain structure for someone—decreeing, for example, "Sally, regardless of what you've *been* wanting, you'd *better* want *this.*"

But how can you know when you are genuinely facilitating someone else's ability to get what they want? In general, they will let you know, most likely by telling you when you are actually helping them, or at least by showing you in some way that they want you to keep trying. That's why Ed Ford suggests that educators should pay respectful attention to students whom they are trying to help become more responsible, and why he recommends *leaving students alone when they don't want help.* The *students* are at the *center* of the process, "calling the shots," letting teachers and administrators know when it is appropriate for them to attempt to aid the students in getting what they—*the students*—want (without, of course, preventing others in the school from getting what they want, as well).

The internalization of Principle 3 could require *considerable* struggling by anyone who has previously internalized competing principles such as "The way to help someone behaving 'badly' is to show them who's boss," or "Children don't know anything and have to be told what they should do," or "I'm responsible for making sure you shape up, so do what I say," or even "I'm your superior because I'm an adult and you're a child, so forget your in-ferior ideas and adopt *my* ideas."

Now you know what I mean by "taking RTP seriously." Having a purely intellectual understanding of that concept is only a first step toward internalizing the principles derived from PCT models, *so they can become functional guides for your day-to-day behavior*. That internalization process might not be easy, and it might not happen quickly, because it just might have to turn your life around! Is it worth the trouble? Yes, if you want to become more capable of assisting your students (and, indeed, anyone else you encounter who needs your help) and to become better able to succeed in applying RTP—*and, more generally and importantly, to succeed in your life.*

Appendix 1
A Primer on PCT

Why is the Responsible Thinking Process so powerful, and why is it so successful with those who are willing to work at reordering their lives? What really goes on inside people as they begin to look within themselves and decide how they want to be? In order to understand the power of this process and what is really taking place inside people during and following the RTP questioning process, it is important to learn how our mind and body interact to achieve our various goals.

Each of us is endowed with a fascinating perceptual system (see the chart on the next page) explained by perceptual control theory (PCT), created by William T. Powers, author of *Behavior: The Control of Perception* and *Making Sense of Behavior*. That system is designed to make sense of our environment so we can build satisfying lives, enabling us to give individual meaning to the world we live in. We fashion this meaning through various systemic levels. Ultimately, there is a highest level where each of us stands as our own person—where "I am the captain of my own ship." Below are brief descriptions of the three highest levels of the perceptual system, which guide who we are and everything we do.

Systems Concepts Level: From this level flow all of the standards and structures we create to have satisfying lives. This is the level where we look within ourselves and establish the way we want to be, how we want to see ourselves as persons, and the kinds of values and beliefs that we believe will bring us happiness. The way we treat others when we are trying to accomplish our goals is reflected in our beliefs and values. And when a person changes how they treat others, this is the level where that change must

CREATING RESPONSIBLE THINKING PROCESS®
FROM PERCEPTUAL CONTROL THEORY
By Edward E. Ford

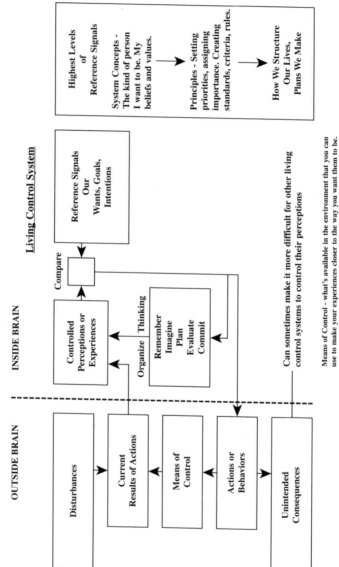

INSIDE BRAIN

Living Control System

OUTSIDE BRAIN

Highest Levels of Reference Signals

System Concepts - The kind of person I want to be. My beliefs and values.

Principles - Setting priorities, assigning importance. Creating standards, criteria, rules.

How We Structure Our Lives, Plans We Make

Reference Signals Our Wants, Goals, Intentions

Compare

Controlled Perceptions or Experiences

Organize Thinking

Remember Imagine Plan Evaluate Commit

Disturbances

Current Results of Actions

Means of Control

Actions or Behaviors

Unintended Consequences

Can sometimes make it more difficult for other living control systems to control their perceptions

Means of Control - what's available in the environment that you can use to make your experiences closer to the way you want them to be.

be internally compatible, or there will be conflict within the changing person's system.

Young children do not have the well-developed understanding of beliefs and values at the Systems Concepts level that adults have. Our understanding of the world develops from our experiences, and our concepts at the higher levels become more sophisticated as we mature. However, young children can say whether they are "happy" or "unhappy," even if they cannot articulate their beliefs and values in detail.

Principles Level: Once we have established how we want to be, it naturally follows that we need to set parameters that define our goals. The Principles level is where we set our priorities and the standards, criteria, and guidelines that establish boundaries on how we should live so as to reflect our values and beliefs. The test for the validity of our standards is our internal satisfaction with how we are living our life. Indeed, we should be able to learn a lot about others from their priorities and standards.

Program Level: In order to live the way we want, based on the criteria we have set, we must have effective programs for accomplishing our goals, so that the plans we make bring us satisfaction. If we want to live in harmony with others, achieving our goals means that we must not violate others' rights. This means that we must not act as disturbances to their attempts to get what they want. So we must each find ways to organize our thinking by creating structured programs, which, when implemented, allow us to accomplish our goals without infringing on the rights of others.

It is at the Program Level where students are helped to resolve their problems by making plans to accomplish their goals without violating the rights of others. Using the PCT chart as a guide, here is a scenario to help explain the various aspects of the PCT model. Further explanations of PCT can be found in the books by Powers mentioned above, in various chapters of *Discipline For Home and School, Book One* and *Book Two*, and in *Freedom From Stress.*

Mathew, a seventh grade student at Rauch Junior High School, was talking to his girlfriend, Emily, outside her third period classroom. The warning bell had rung. His room was down the hall. Emily smiled, giggled, and then went into her classroom. Mathew took off on a run, wanting not to be late for his class. Mrs. Kuhn, standing outside her classroom by which he was running, called to Mathew, "Stop running!"

Mrs. Kuhn saw Mathew violating a school safety rule: "No running in the halls." Mathew, on the other hand, wanted to be on time to his class. Herein lies the first step to an understanding of PCT. Mathew's *Reference Signals* or *Goals* were two: he wanted a few precious moments with Emily, the current love of his life, and he also wanted to be on time to class. Mrs. Kuhn, on the other hand, was charged with monitoring the hall in her classroom area, and she saw Mathew running—his *Actions*.

As living control systems, we are not aware of exactly what goes on *inside* the brains of others. In all the school discipline programs of which I'm aware, the *Actions* of others are what educators attempt to change. And how do they try to change them? By acting as *Disturbances*. They try to do something to students—punishments, rewards, threats, or criticism—to try to get them to change their *Actions*. In Mathew's case, Mrs. Kuhn could have stopped him, lectured him, or written him up, or, because she had caught him running on numerous occasions, she could have sent him to the office. If she did any of these things, Mrs. Kuhn would be dealing with what she "saw" Mathew doing, his *Actions*. Mathew, on the other hand, was trying to arrange a way of satisfying two apparently incompatible *Goals*, time with Emily and getting to class on time. At the moment Emily left him to go into her class, he *Perceived* himself at a great distance from where he needed to be at the time, and he *Acted* to correct that situation.

The *Current Results of Behavior* are what Mathew actually was accomplishing: staying with his girlfriend and making it hard for himself to get to class on time. That's what his *Actions* were accomplishing. One of the results was *close* to the result he wanted: he wanted to stay with his girlfriend, and he was doing so. The other result was *far* from what he wanted to accomplish: he wanted to get to class on time, but he had stayed too long and was too far from the class to do so. Thus, he created a problem with Mrs. Kuhn by breaking a rule and getting her unwelcome attention.

Supposing Mrs. Kuhn, using the RTP questioning process, had called to Mathew, "Mathew, what are you doing?" He might have looked at her, stopped running, and then said, "I'm trying to get to class on time." (Notice he stated what he wanted to accomplish—his *Goal*, not what Mrs. Kuhn saw him doing—his *Actions*.) Then he might have continued to his class, walking at a fast clip. Later, Mrs. Kuhn might have mentioned to Mathew that she often saw him running in the hall, and then she might have asked him whether running in the hall is against the rules. If he acknowledged such, she might have asked him if that was going to get him into more trouble, and, if so, would he like to work on solving this problem. She was obviously willing to teach him how to *organize* his *thinking* (see page 68). If he saw her as sincere and willing to help him solve his dilemma, or, to put it in PCT terms, to be a *Means of Control*, Mrs. Kuhn would be helping Mathew by using the techniques of RTP. She would be asking him to look within himself (at the higher levels described above), decide how he wanted to be (in this case, to live within the rules or to continue violating the rules), and then learn how to structure his life such that he could accomplish his *Goals* without violating the rights of others. His plan might include setting a better time to leave his girlfriend, so he could be on time to class without breaking school rules, and arranging for other times to visit with her.

Reorganization: Whenever there is a conflict within our perceptual system, such as when there are conflicting beliefs or standards, our system senses the conflict and eventually might begin to reorganize itself, generating random signals that suggest various ways that might resolve the conflict. Some of these ways, if applied, might reduce the conflict, many would not. When we ultimately come up with a way to reduce conflict sufficiently or eliminate it entirely, reorganization stops. This might require considerable time, during which the reorganizing person is likely to feel angry, anxious, and/or depressed. RTP is designed to support children who are experiencing reorganization. And through the use of the questioning process, RTP teaches them how to look within themselves, think through the consequences of various possible changes in their reorganizing perceptual systems, and decide how they want to be. (For a more detailed explanation of reorganization, see *Freedom From Stress* by Ed Ford, Chapter 7, "Reorganization: The Mind's Repair Kit"; also see Chapter 6.)

I once asked a sixth grader who was punching other students who teased him whether punching was allowed, and he said, "No." Then I asked, "Does it make things better?" He answered, "No, I keep getting into trouble." Showing frustration, he added, "But what else can I do?" Using a "chill out" pass to leave conflict-producing situations by going to a protected environment, until he was able to calm down, provided the support he needed for successful reorganization. He began to avoid confrontations and found more peace within himself.

Resolving Conflicts: We all want to be at peace within ourselves, with values and beliefs that are in harmony with each other and are in harmony with the ways we have prioritized them and the standards we have set. We might not be able to articulate the best ways things should be, but we certainly feel conflict when we sense inconsistencies between our beliefs and priorities, and the ways we are currently dealing with our lives. When we are angry, anxious, or depressed, indicating internal conflict, we must ultimately resolve our conflicts at a higher harmonious level in order to restore internal peace. To quote William Powers, "When there is conflict, whether between people or inside oneself, lasting change can take place only if there is stability and harmony at the next higher level." I have heard him say this many times, but only recently did I really think through the implications.

If my wife, Hester, wants to take a walk somewhere other than where we have been going regularly, and I would rather stay where we regularly walk, I sense the conflict. The conflict is at the Program level. Considering the situation at the Principles level, I say to myself, "Really, Ed, what's more important, enjoying time with your wife, or where you enjoy it?" To me, the answer is obvious, and so we go where Hester wants. Going up to the Principles level has enabled me to resolve the conflict.

I know of a couple who had very serious problems in their marriage. The wife left and moved to an apartment. The husband stayed home with the children, determined to keep the family going and to work things out. Eventually, the wife returned, and they did work things out. As the husband told me later, for him, divorce was never an option. He had resolved the issue at the Systems Concepts level: "marriage is sacred" was a value he had set at that level.

When I had a family counseling practice, I remember working with a woman whose career frequently took her out of town. She told me she had almost lost everything most important to her—her husband and her children. Her husband, a busy executive, struggled to maintain family life both in the evenings and on the weekends when his wife was absent. One of their sons developed very disruptive behavior at an early age. The way the woman was structuring her life resulted in conflict. But then she reflected at the Principles level and decided that having more time alone with her husband and being a more important part of her children's lives had much higher priorities than her job. So she took a part-time job working out of her home.

In many cases, single parents greatly desire adult relationships. When such a relationship develops, the time they spend with their children is reduced. As the parent becomes aware of this and tries to spend more time with the children, the new adult partner experiences a reduction in time with the parent, and conflict arises. The parent can resolve the conflict at the Principles level by examining priorities. Which is really more important to the single parent, spending time with the children or the adult relationship? Attempting to satisfy both areas in the conflict often just makes things worse.

When we work out ways to resolve conflicts, it is critical that our plans be in harmony with our values and priorities. The RTP questioning process provides support for eliminating internal conflicts by teaching people to look within themselves and decide how they ought to be.

We each create the kind of person we want to be, and when we get married, some of us foolishly create expectations for ourselves about the kinds of persons we want those around us to be. But when we try to change others to meet our expectations, they often see our attempts as lacking in respect and very controlling. In serious relationships, such attempts might be seen as a lack of committed love. People are not designed to have their goals set by others, but to set and satisfy their own goals. In all situations in which we find ourselves with others, in order to satisfy our own goals, we must learn to respect the rights of those around us—otherwise we are likely to interfere with the attempts of others to satisfy their own goals.

Quality Time: The real key to building a strong, lasting, and enjoyable relationship between two people is quality time. This type of interactive time alone together on a daily basis will not only build and maintain confidence in their mutual ability to resolve differences, but, more importantly, it will help raise the level of importance each individual ascribes to the other when reflecting on which priorities are most important. I have found in the many schools in which I have worked that, universally, chronically disruptive students totally lack quality time with anyone. I know of many programs bringing volunteers into schools to spend time with such students that have had remarkable results in helping those students turn their lives around.

For the first time, there are others who really care enough to show an interest and spend interactive time with them on a regular basis (see Appendix 4).

Using RTP on Ourselves: I have been working with work-furlough prisoners at one of our sheriff's jails. They are at their jobs each weekday and then spend the rest of their days and nights in jail. I teach a class on responsible thinking. The first night of the class, I ask the prisoners individually to list approximately five things that are really important to them. These might include friends, spouse, children, education, sobriety, health, job, God, faith, and so forth. Then I ask them to prioritize the items they have listed. Many of them begin to reflect for the first time in their lives on what is really important to them and whether there are conflicts among the items they have selected.

Often, the following week, prior to class, several of the prisoners tell me that their reflections on priorities have changed their lives. And in my conversations with them after the six- to eight-week class is over, some say this was the most important thing they did in the class.

I now realize that the profound changes many of these inmates went through are similar to the changes many students experience with RTP. And I think that what happens in those students also happens in many administrators and teachers using RTP. They reflect on their situations at a level where there is harmony, and the result is a resolution of their conflicts. Those who take longer to resolve their conflicts apparently either have a hard time establishing priorities or must give up goals that are hard to give up.

It now seems obvious to me that if you want to experience what your student or spouse or child is going through, and what many educators *do on their own as a result of using this process when working with students*, then the real key to understanding what the use of RTP offers is to *use the process on yourself*.

Taking this a step further, I now realize that in my twenty-five years of doing professional counseling, I have had little to do with individuals resolving their own conflicts, other than asking questions that helped them look within themselves and decide how they want to be, and then offering, from my own experience, ways of structuring their lives to satisfy their goals. Also, I believe I helped some of them move up to a level at which they found harmony and could resolve their conflicts. I needed to stay out of their way as they went through this process, allowing them the freedom to work within themselves and not getting in their way by telling them what I thought they needed.

If you want to get an idea of what it is like to "look within yourself and decide if the way you are is the way you want to be," the first thing to do is to make a list of the things in life that are important to you. Included on such a list might be children, spouse, parents, extended family, close friends, other specific individuals, pets, habits like smoking and drinking, work, hobbies, health, faith, home, certain possessions, etc. Then try arranging the items in order of importance, from highest priority to lowest. Perhaps you might discover that the things you seem to spend the most time doing and the people with whom you spend the most time are rated a lot lower in importance than other things you ignore and people with whom you spend very little time.

If you want less conflict in your life, this is where real change begins. As you begin to look within yourself in this way, you become better equipped to understand where change needs to happen, and then you can restructure your life accordingly. I myself have done this. At times, I have had to "look within myself" and deal with what I needed to change. I sometimes needed to decide whether taking on another task was more important than the time I was giving up with someone important to me. This can have an especially powerful effect on a person whose own life has been in shambles, as I learned from many of the inmates at the jail. This has been an earth-shaking experience for many of them.

It is no easy task to take a long, hard look within yourself, reflect on whether this is really the way you want to be, and make sure that the way you have structured your priorities is bringing you the happiness you want. But only you can look within yourself. No one else can. No one can even make suggestions as to how your priorities should be arranged. Only *you* can know if how you have created your internal world is reducing or producing internal conflict.

Once done, as many teachers and administrators have found out, this offers a personal understanding of the experience that many students, especially the more chronically disrupting ones, go through. Educators who have found that their lives profoundly change after having used this process *have used the questioning process that they have been using with students on themselves*. As they begin to look seriously within themselves, they sense the same transformation in their own lives that they have seen in some of their students. Thus, this experience is not just for disruptive children—it can happen within all of us.

Attempting to Control the Behavior of Others: Trying to control what we hear and see other people say and do is futile. Students must learn efficient ways to deal with internal conflict, just as they must learn how to solve school-work problems efficiently. Trying to control them by giving either "rewards" or "punishments" does *not* teach them how to deal with conflict within themselves. Instead, it acts as a disturbance to their systems, and (to paraphrase B. F. Skinner) they will likely attempt to *counter-control* whoever tries to control them. They might even try to make would-be controllers angry or harm them physically. (To learn more, visit www.responsiblethinking.com and read the section entitled "PCT, Reinforcement Theory, Counter-control, and RTP," by Tom Bourbon.)

In general, what we see another person do gives us little indication of the various beliefs and standards within that person. A child might scream in bed for "a drink of water," but that action could have more to do with getting a good-night hug and kiss. Or a child running down the hall to class might be mainly concerned with getting to class on time, while a teacher is mainly concerned about safety risks. We cannot expect to understand *completely* others' experiences and how they are organized at their highest levels. Consider how you feel when people criticize what they *think* you are doing, or laugh at what they *believe* you mean. *You* understand what you are doing or meaning, based directly on your inner experiences, but others can only *guess*, based on your actions. So when someone tries to control another person by "rewarding" or "punishing" them, they could easily be completely mistaken about what is "rewarding" or "punishing," thus creating conflict and chaos. Rather, people should be treated as living control systems designed to resolve their own internal conflicts. And the real reward for disruptive students is internal—the peace they experience and the growing belief and confidence in their ability to resolve their own conflicts successfully. RTC teachers are often seen by students as the persons who believe in them and their ability to make it.

Becoming More Responsible: Students who are having problems getting along with their peers will find little peace and satisfaction in their lives unless they learn to resolve their conflicts at the next higher level by creating ways of reaching their goals *without being in conflict with others.* They must learn to look within themselves and find ways of satisfying their goals while living in harmony with others. This is what happens when RTP is used properly. It is designed to teach them to be sensitive to differences between the standards of wherever they are and what they are doing. It is also designed to teach them how to get what they want without violating the rights of others, through plan making. This means learning how to structure their lives so that they do not act as disturbances to others when they try to get what they want. They must become aware of the beliefs or values and resulting standards of where they are. All communities have rules, and to live without conflict, these rules must be learned and followed. What is the purpose of rules? To provide standards to be followed by all people who live in the same environment, so that they can achieve their goals and get what they want, while at the same time being minimal disturbances to others. *This is what responsibility is all about.*

Thus, three things are essential to keep in mind when helping children to become more responsible. First, any attempt to control students is antagonistic to how they are designed and to their learning to think responsibly. Second, for a discipline process to be effective, those using it must treat students the same way as those having difficulty in an academic subject: in a non-punitive, non-controlling atmosphere, with understanding, respect, and patience. Third, students need to be taught to look within themselves and decide how they want to be, and then how to structure ways of achieving their goals. This includes being taught how to make plans that will help them resolve their own conflicts and work with others to resolve mutual differences in ways that do not violate the standards and rules of the environment in which they find themselves.

Appendix 2
RTP Flow Chart

The purpose of this chart is to give educators an overall idea of how the process works, and what happens when students disrupt. *It is merely an outline—Discipline for Home and School, Book One* and *Book Two* should be used as training manuals by all who implement the process. The detailed instructional materials in those two books were developed to guide educators in using RTP properly, maintaining the integrity of the process.

Many mistakes are possible due to the lack of adequate preparation prior to implementing the process. For example, some teachers might use the questioning techniques to attempt to "control" their students, while others might use those techniques selectively (perhaps with Tom Troublemaker, but not with Sweet Sally). Or a student might be sent home directly from a classroom following a series of minor disruptions, even though the decision to send a student home is supposed to be made only in the Responsible Thinking Classroom, with the approval and support of the school administrator, and the only time students are sent home other than due to disrupting in the RTC is following a *serious* act of misconduct, as defined by the school district's governing board. Studying both *Book 1* and *Book 2* is *essential* for gaining an adequate understanding of RTP for implementing the process correctly.

RTP FLOW CHART

Serious Acts of Misconduct

Student commits a serious act of misconduct and is sent immediately to the RTC or the appropriate administrator.

Student is given a board mandated suspension from school and returns, or student returns to school after having disrupted in the RTC and been sent home. He and his parents or guardian meet with the school administrator to determine if there is a commitment to follow the rules.

If student still refuses to follow the rules, he returns home until he is ready. If he is ready to follow rules, he is then sent to the RTC teacher to work on a plan to become responsible within the school environment.

School Bus

Student creates a safety hazard on the bus and the driver asks the RTP questions. If the student continues to disrupt, he is again asked the RTP questions, then goes to the front seat of the bus, which is used as RTC. The driver notifies dispatch to notify the student's principal and parents that the student is in danger of losing his right to ride the bus. If the student continues to disrupt, he can no longer ride the bus until he returns with a plan and negotiates with the bus driver.

Disruptions

Student disrupts and is asked the RTP questions by his teacher.

Student settles down and creates no further disruptions.

Student disrupts in RTC and the RTC teacher asks the RTP questions. If he continues to disrupt, the RTC teacher fills out a referral form. He is then taken to the office and either sent home or other appropriate action is taken.

Non-Compliant Students

Any time the student is non-compliant and refuses to deal with the teacher, a referral form is filled out and the student is sent immediately to the RTC. If student refuses to go to the RTC, an administrator is called to remove student.

Chill-Out Plans

As part of a student's previous plan to deal with their anger or other emotional problems, a Chill-Out Plan is often used. This allows him to use the RTC as a place to calm down and then return to where he belongs.

Intervention Team

Call an intervention team meeting when there is an increase in disruptions, specific types of disruptions, and/or any other concerns about the student.

Later, student disrupts again and is asked "What are you doing?", "What did you say would happen the next time you disrupted?", and "Where do you need to be now?". Teacher fills out the referral form and sends student to RTC.

Student arrives at RTC, signs in, hands RTC teacher his referral form and if new to RTC, process is explained. He is assigned a seat.

When student is ready to return to where he then belongs, he fills out his plan. Student and RTC teacher review plan, making any needed changes.

Once plan is approved by RTC teacher, student returns to school routine when return does not create a disruption. Student negotiates plan with teacher as soon as practical. If student disrupts while waiting to negotiate with his teacher, the student is asked "What are you doing?", "What happens when you disrupt while waiting to negotiate?", and "Where do you need to be now?". The student returns to the RTC and RTC is notified of this by the teacher. The student must now wait until the teacher is available outside normal classroom time.

Student explains plan to teacher. If teacher is not satisfied with plan, she offers alternatives. Once readmitted to class, student returns completed plan to RTC for permanent files.

Please Note: The word *TEACHER* is used to denote all certified and classified staff including those not working on school grounds, such as bus drivers.

Appendix 3
Responsible Thinking Process Card

RESPONSIBLE THINKING PROCESS (RTP)®
www.responsiblethinking.com

By Edward E. Ford – based on perceptual control theory

Copyright 2004 by Edward E. Ford and RTP, Inc.

For children to succeed, they must believe you care, and you have confidence in their ability to solve problems. Always ask questions, in a respectful, calm, curious voice. Never punish, reward, lecture, or yell, because trying to control another doesn't work. Avoid excuses, don't ask why. When they disrupt, ask:

- **WHAT ARE YOU DOING?**
- **WHAT ARE THE RULES? or IS THAT OK?**
- **WHAT HAPPENS WHEN YOU BREAK THE RULES?**
- **IS THIS WHAT YOU WANT TO HAPPEN?**
- **WHAT DO YOU WANT TO DO NOW?**
- **WHAT WILL HAPPEN IF YOU DISRUPT AGAIN?**

WHEN CHILDREN AVOID DEALING WITH YOU

If they avoid answering a question, repeat it. If they persist in not dealing with you, then ask:

DO YOU WANT TO WORK ON THIS OR NOT?

If they continue to avoid dealing with you, then you say:

YOU NEED TO GO TO THE RTC.

or, if after settling down, later on they again begin to disrupt, then you ask: **WHAT ARE YOU DOING?**
WHAT DID YOU SAY WOULD HAPPEN THE NEXT TIME YOU DISRUPTED?
WHERE DO YOU NEED TO GO NOW?

<u>Once you have said this, never back down.</u> The child must leave at once and go to the RTC. When they want to return and obey the rules, they must create a detailed plan and use this plan to negotiate with the person in charge of where they were disrupting. After attempting to create a plan, they review it with the RTC teacher.

NEGOTIATING PLANS IMPORTANT TO PROCESS

When children approach a teacher or parent to negotiate their way back to where they were disrupting, they should be given time to explain how they are going to deal with the problem the next time it occurs. This should take about 3 to 5 minutes. If part of their plan is unacceptable, alternatives should be offered. Their plan should never be ignored or refused. Negotiating is critical to building student-teacher relationships. As a reminder for students to use their plans, ask: ARE YOU FOLLOWING YOUR PLAN? DO YOU WANT TO CHANGE YOUR PLAN?

AFTER NEGOTIATING PLAN, STUDENT DISRUPTS AGAIN

Ask: WHAT ARE YOU DOING? ARE YOU FOLLOWING

YOUR PLAN? WHAT HAPPENS IF YOU DON'T FOLLOW YOUR PLAN?

DEALING WITH CHRONICALLY DISRUPTIVE CHILDREN
Call an intervention team meeting. The team's purpose is NOT to decide what to DO to the student to get him to CHANGE his BEHAVIOR. Rather, the team's purpose is to offer the kind of support that would enable the child both to look within himself and decide how he wants to be based on his priorities and standards, and then to create a plan that will help him manage his own life in a way that "doesn't violate the rights of others." The team should meet without the child, but should be made up of those who have spent time with the child. They try to discover from others what is important to the child, and the designated team members create a plan of support to be offered the child.

HOW TO CREATE AN EFFECTIVE PLAN
This process helps them organize their thinking, and builds the self-discipline and self-confidence necessary to resolve future conflicts. 1. Work on one specific problem at a time. 2. Set a measurable goal. 3. Ask how they are going to deal with this problem the next time it happens, then explain, in detail, specifically how they will work toward achieving a measurable goal. 4. Create a chart or monitor form as an aid to achieving their goal. 5. They should find someone to whom they can report their progress.

QUALITY TIME: THE KEY TO STRONG RELATIONS
The stronger the relationship, the fewer your disagreements and differences. Nothing builds a relationship like quality time.

CRITERIA FOR QUALITY TIME
1. DO ACTIVITIES THAT PROMOTE AWARENESS OF EACH OTHER AND CREATE PLEASURE THROUGH MUTUAL EFFORT through interactive activities such as playing games, exercising or working together, taking a walk or riding a bike. NOT passive activities such as watching TV or movies, just being together, or physical intimacy. These activities do not create strong relationships, but only enhance a committed love that already exists. 2. DO QUALITY TIME ACTIVITIES ALONE TOGETHER, NOT WITH OTHERS. 3. DO YOUR ACTIVITIES ON A REGULAR BASIS. A minimum goal for adults should be 30 minutes a day, five days a week, 20 minutes per day with children. Commitment guarantees a close intimacy.

TO ORDER BOOKS, VIDEOS, AND CARDS:
CONTACT: WWW.BRANDTPUBLISHING.COM
RTP, 10209 N 56th St., Scottsdale, AZ 85253 Ph 480-991-4860

To receive three copies of the card reproduced here, send a stamped self-addressed envelope to RTP, Inc., 10209 N. 56th St., Scottsdale, AZ 85253.

Appendix 4
Quality Time

Whenever someone is having problems with a child, regardless of the circumstances, the first question that should be asked is how much *quality time* those who are important to the child have been spending with him. Anyone's ability to resolve problems, to stand firm in the face of adversity, and to work through difficult conflicts depends on the strength that comes from personal relationships out of which develops a strong belief in self. Disruption and acting out are symptomatic of a fundamental problem: insecurity fed by the loneliness that comes from a lack of warm, caring, joyful relationships.

From my experience in working with families and consulting in schools, corrections, mental health, and residential treatment centers over many years, plus raising my own eight children, I believe that nothing is more important than our individual alone time with our spouse and with each of our children. Children create their perceptions of their parents based on the time they have spent with them and the *quality* of that time. We all tend to listen to and respect those whom we perceive respect us, who care about us, and have expressed, both verbally and by their actions, a belief that we have worth as a human being.

What gives a teacher or parent true access to children is when the children believe that whoever is working with them cares about them and, more importantly, believes in their ability to resolve their problems. If you don't have confidence in your children's ability to succeed, they'll know it, and that lack of belief will very likely translate into your children's lack of confidence in themselves. Thus, the most important step when teaching responsible thinking involves spending the kind of time that is going to create this belief on the part of children that someone cares about them. I call this *quality time*. This is discussed in detail in my books *Love Guaranteed* and *Freedom From Stress*.

With this belief in themselves, children are able to commit to themselves not only a promise to resolve their problems, but also to do so *cooperatively with those who spend individual alone time with them*. Over the past 30 years, I have taught couples and parents with children how to build sufficient strength in their marriages and families so that they could resolve their problems in reasonable and rational ways. Quality time is the only effective process I've found that will create the kind of love and trust needed for relationships to survive and grow.

From perceptual control theory, I have learned that we create our perception of others from mutual, interactive types of experiences that people have with each other. The criteria for these experiences are as follows: first, whatever you do, you must be *aware* of each other; second, you must create the enjoyment, rather than passively watch TV or a movie; third, you must spend this time *alone together* with whomever you are trying to build a relationship; and fourth, this activity should happen on a *daily or regular basis*.

The success stories using quality time are many. I once had a single parent tell me that she had never had a day's problem with her 18-year-old son. The boy's father had left her prior to her son's birth. She said to me, "When my son first began to walk, I resolved right then that he and I would take a walk every day of our lives together." And she added, "We've done that. Many times he'd come home from school and he'd say to me, 'Come on, Mom, we gotta take our walk.'"

The greatest story of all was during a group meeting with former prison inmates, on probation. I was running these groups for Jake Jacobs, an adult probation officer. I had asked the group members what were the toughest problems they had on probation. Most talked about disagreements with their spouses or live-in friends. One man whom I will call Charlie said that he had been doing well with his girlfriend for the past three months. When I asked what he was doing, he said, "We take a long walk every night." I asked how he figured this out. He pointed to Jake and said, "He gave me this card on quality time. It said you had to take a walk, and that's what I've been doing." Charlie had been a drug addict since he was eight years old. He was then 38 and had been a recovering addict for two years. He'd been in and out of prison many times, gone through two marriages, and had, in succession, lived with and beaten up 15 to 20 women. A year after he told me this, he was still succeeding with his girlfriend. He invited Jake and myself to his wedding but had to delay it because he wanted his son, who was in prison, to be best man. Today, Charlie is married, is still taking his walks, and is still doing well.

Over the years, as I was developing my ideas on quality time, I never realized that the best example was right under my own nose. I'm speaking of my lovely wife, Hester. It was only after our grandchildren began to appear that I became conscious of how she really worked with children. As they would arrive at our home for a visit or an overnight stay, no sooner would they be in the door than she would be down on the floor with them, doing a puzzle, coloring a picture, playing a card game, or figuring out the rules of a board game. Or she would be off on a bike ride, or taking a walk down the street, or having a tea party, or creating something in the kitchen. She takes children to her poster shop, and there they answer the phone, or help my son, Thomas, who runs the framing department. Hester set up an area in her store for children, with a small table and chair, and with blocks and other creative toys with which they can play while their parents are shopping around. Often, when their parents want to leave, the children want to stay and play.

For outings, Hester takes children to the train park, or to the zoo, or to one of the local art museums, or to climb one of the many mountains around Phoenix. My daughter Dorothy does the same with her three children. The rest of the family claims that she's the only mother who is going to wear out her children! She's always on the move, and she and her husband, Eric, constantly expose their children to the many experiences that can enhance a child's world.

Thus, the key to raising children has to do with *creating an atmosphere* in which youngsters are likely to obey rules and to learn to think responsibly, and their parents, in turn, have access to working with them. Quality time is the only kind of activity that will create that kind of atmosphere. This also means that not only must parents set rules and standards that reflect the parents' own values and beliefs, but they must follow through with the natural restrictions that flow from refusal to follow rules. In turn, all children eventually must learn to respect the rules of the culture in which they live, or they will be in conflict with the people in that culture. My experience with my own children has taught me that children tend to adopt the standards and values of their parents *if they've established a close, loving relationship with them, and if the choices they have made that reflect those values and standards in the home have brought them a satisfying life.* Ultimately, if children perceive you as caring about them, as believing in them, and if they recognize the existence of reasonable standards within the home, they are more likely to work cooperatively to find a way to get along.